High Impact Philanthropy

WILEY NONPROFIT LAW, FINANCE, AND MANAGEMENT SERIES

High Impact Philanthropy

HOW DONORS, BOARDS, AND
NONPROFIT ORGANIZATIONS
CAN TRANSFORM COMMUNITIES

Kay Sprinkel Grace
Alan L. Wendroff

JOHN WILEY & SONS, INC.

NEW YORK • CHICHESTER • WEINHEIM • BRISBANE • SINGAPORE • TORONTO

Copyright © 2001 by John Wiley and Sons, Inc. All rights reserved.

Published simultaneously in Canada.

This publication is designed to provide accurate and authoritative information in regard to the subject matter covered. It is sold with the understanding that the publisher is not engaged in rendering legal, accounting, or other professional services. If legal advice or other expert assistance is required, the services of a competent professional person should be sought.

Library of Congress Cataloging-in-Publication Data
Grace, Kay Sprinkel.
　　High impact philanthropy : how donors, boards, and nonprofit organizations can transform communities / Kay Sprinkel Grace, Alan L. Wendroff.
　　　　p. cm. — (Wiley nonprofit law, finance, and management series)
　　ISBN 0-471-36918-7 (cloth : alk. paper)
　　1. Fund raising.　2. Nonprofit organizations—Finance.
3. Endowments.　4. Community foundations.　I. Wendroff, Alan L.　II. Title.　III. Series.

HV41.2 .B43 2001
658.15′224—dc21   00-061964

Printed in the United States of America.

10　9　8　7　6　5　4　3　2　1

High Impact Philanthropy is dedicated to the founders of Sage Hill School in Orange County, California. Their commitment to values-based philanthropy has inspired new levels of transformational giving. The school will stand for generations as a testimony to what people with a dream can accomplish when they understand the power and impact of community investment. My royalties from the book are my gift to Sage Hill School, and are given with gratitude for the opportunity to be present at the creation of this remarkable institution.

This book is also dedicated to my professional colleagues around the world who have listened to me as I developed many of these ideas, and especially to Myrna Hall, Vice President for Development at the University of Colorado at Boulder, with whom the original seeds were planted.

KSG

To Lyllian, my best advisor for more than 33 years—this book could not have been written without your constant support and love. All my love.

For Kathy and David, my children, and for Debbi, my niece, for your constant words of love and encouragement.

ALW

Contents

About the Authors

Kay Sprinkel Grace, CFRE, is an internationally acclaimed independent consultant, speaker, facilitator, and writer. She has also been a core faculty member of the Fund Raising School since 1980. After successful careers in journalism and education, she became a development professional in 1979, working in several organizations before starting her own consulting firm in 1987. Since then, she has worked as trainer or consultant with thousands of nonprofit volunteers and professionals in the areas of board and staff leadership, planning, and capital and annual fund raising. More than 35 years as a volunteer—principally for Stanford University, where she received her BA and MA degrees and where she has been honored for her fund-raising leadership—add perspective to this book. She is the author of *Beyond Fund Raising: New Strategies for Innovation and Investment in Non-profits,* also published by John Wiley & Sons, Inc. (1997). She and her husband, Stanford classmate Geoffrey Beaumont, live in San Francisco.

Alan L. Wendroff, CFRE, is an independent consultant specializing in counseling nonprofit organizations in fund-raising and management issues. He teaches at California State University–Hayward in the extended education department; he also gives workshops and seminars, and lectures extensively in the San Francisco Bay Area where he makes his home. He is a member of the National Society of Fund Raising Executives and the San Francisco Development Executives Roundtable. He is the author of *Special Events: Proven Strategies for Nonprofit Fund Raising,* also published by John Wiley & Sons, Inc.

Preface

The time for this book is now. Rapid changes in the economy, shifts in donor demographics, and greater participation in community issues by people and institutions not previously involved in philanthropy have combined to position nonprofits around the world at the crossroads of opportunity and challenge. Transformational giving, the core of high impact philanthropy, can change lives, institutions, and communities.

The opportunities are great:

- Human and social needs are on the increase, and the sense of community responsibility toward these issues is more acute than ever. Government support is declining: From higher education to grass-roots human services, the shortfall has been felt and communities are responding. Nonprofits are uniquely positioned to be the vehicles through which vast societal changes can occur.
- Greater wealth has been generated in the past decade than ever before in the history of the world. Portions of the population inexperienced with wealth are finding they have the time and the resources to invest in causes and communities. Many want to become engaged deeply with the values-based issues they care about.
- Nonprofits have matured, incorporating sound practices from the business sector into their management and leadership. In many areas nonprofits still need to strengthen their accountability and response. However, significant progress has been made in the past several decades toward achieving greater respect from donors and volunteers. There is more community awareness of the importance of the nonprofit sector; and more appreciation for its impact on social, human, cultural, and artistic needs.

The challenges, however, are many:

- Nonprofits must position their marketing and outreach efforts around the issues they are enhancing (such as greater access for children to the arts, better healthcare for seniors) or the issues they are solving (such as teen pregnancy, or orphans in the United States and abroad who need foster or permanent families). People investing now in their communities are interested first in issues, and second in the institutions or organizations that address those issues. Because many people are so new to philanthropy, they are unfamiliar with the names of organizations. All they know is that they want to invest in the issues that relate to their values: education, health, social justice, or the cultural enhancement of their communities. This calls for a change in nonprofit marketing—an area covered in depth in this book.
- The need for leadership in the nonprofit sector is critical. Competition from the for-profit sector for talented people is strong. A robust economy and low unemployment in the beginning of the twenty-first century have thinned the ranks of available nonprofit staff leaders. The literature of the profession has addressed this need repeatedly, citing dozens of examples of organizations whose searches for top-quality development or executive directors were long and fruitless. To attract the best-quality leaders into top jobs, and the most talented students into degree or certificate programs, the nonprofit sector must reconsider its self-image as "charity," looking upon itself instead as a critical broker in effecting community change. This is also a key element in attracting transformational gifts. In business schools and public policy programs, nonprofits should constitute an equal career alternative. Salaries, which have improved substantially, must become even more competitive. Relationships between boards and staffs, often a strain to both, can benefit from evaluation and rethinking. Otherwise, good people will continue to leave the sector in frustration or, hearing or sensing these issues, never enter nonprofit employment. When this happens, it is not only the organizations that suffer: Communities lose the dynamic leadership they need to partner with visionary institutions.
- The singular lack of community vision for the role and importance of nonprofits in the arts, culture, social and human services, and education continues to plague the sector, leading to a balkanization of organizations that should be working together to fulfill the broad agenda of civic, corporate, and nonprofit leaders. In some communities, these attempts have flowered; in others, they have either begun and failed or have never happened. The nonprofit sector can be a leader in pushing an agenda

with an issues-based vision that requires organizations to work together to address community needs.

- Maintaining the optimism to be partners in change is a constant challenge for nonprofits. Lack of funding, turnover in leadership, contentious issues between boards and staffs, and other problems are chronic. Mission drift (Grace, 1997) creeps slowly within organizations until they realize that their excessive focus on organizational issues has distanced them from their mission. Confidence in the sector erodes, and the case for partnering dims.
- Lack of information, and even misinformation, still distances nonprofits from potential donor-investors. To bridge this gulf, nonprofits need to add community education about philanthropy to their agendas. At every opportunity, through their marketing, donor development and fund development programs, they need to position the power and impact of this sector in the most positive possible light. Skepticism and misunderstanding about what the sector can accomplish, and how we work as organizations, could be minimized by promotion of our achievements. Too often, the public only hears about the abuses in the sector. We need to let them know the ways in which we are having an impact, why we are the most appropriate vehicle for accomplishing change and gaining results, and how they can become confident investors in our sector.

High Impact Philanthropy was written to guide organizations into these opportunities and through these challenges so they can be both attractive to donors, and ready to use and manage effectively the transformational gifts they receive. These gifts, defined in Chapter 1 but understood intuitively by those who hear the term, make all the difference.

This book is intended for nonprofit organizations, their investors, their governing bodies, and their professional staffs, each of which is a vital partner in enhancing communities through the strengthening of institutions. The result is a heightened capacity to address issues effectively. It is about transformation in giving, in organizations, and in communities.

It is about the future of philanthropy, and the wave on which we are all already riding.

Kay Sprinkel Grace
San Francisco, California
October 2000

Philanthropy is now a regular feature in the news media. When the yearly report of how much is given to nonprofits is published by the Giving

USA/AAFRC Trust for Philanthropy, it is covered by all media from newspapers, to television, radio and the Internet.

News coverage that the nonprofit sector had to beg for only five or six years ago is now common in the media. On July 6, 2000, the business section of the *New York Times* featured an article titled "New Philanthropists Put Donations to Work: Shifting Away From Aiding Big Charities." The article's lead sentence, "It isn't his father's philanthropy," explains one of the reasons we wrote this book. Throughout this book you will read about how the "new philanthropists" want to transform the world, and their communities, through giving—not only of money but also of their time and expertise. High impact philanthropy can be achieved only by a transformational donor-investor.

The July 24th issue of the weekly newsmagazine *TIME* featured "The New Philanthropists" as its cover story. The secondary title read, "They're hands on. They want results. Who gives, and how much." At the top of the cover were photographs of six philanthropists who had made gifts between $2 million and $22 billion. Their stories were part of the cover article. Most nonprofit agencies are so far from receiving grants or gifts from these philanthropists that one wonders why anyone who works for, or volunteers for, a nonprofit agency should read the article. What good could accrue to the nonprofit sector from stories about multi-million-billion-aires?

The potential good is that non–million-billion-aires like to read about people who have such enormous wealth; they like to know where such people donate their money. It is a motivational factor for donor-investors who can give, but a somewhat lesser amount.

In the *TIME* article, Stacy Palmer, editor of the *Chronicle of Philanthropy* (the leading newspaper of the nonprofit world), is quoted as asking, "Are charitable organizations ready to deal with all that money?" She goes on to ask the billion-dollar question, ". . . [Do] you have the people in place to do the work[?]." The answer, of course, is that the majority of nonprofits don't; just look at the employment-opportunity pages of the *Chronicle*. This is the other reason we wrote this book: to show the nonprofit organization how to recruit for, create, and maintain a major gifts culture. Like the authors of this book, Stacy Palmer wants to build a platform from which the nonprofit can take advantage of the largesse that may come its way. The nonprofit can use that funding to address the issues, but only if it has recruited a board of directors and a professional staff who in turn have built a development and programmatic team that will put the agency to work in the local, regional, national, or international community. Thomas L. Friedman, in his recent book, *The Lexus and the Olive Tree: Understanding Globalization,* explains how the world has grown much smaller and, with advanced communications, much more interconnected. The relationship between the world and its many countries is like the relationship between a large city and one of its neighborhoods. Friedman goes on to explain how the economy of one smaller country can have a domino effect on the economy of the entire world. This effect, if it is negative, can ultimately lessen philanthropic donations in all nations, especially the United States. Conversely, the nonprofit sector will gain if the effect is positive. Either way, individual nonprofits must be prepared for what takes place. *High Impact Philanthropy* was written to help nonprofits—from the largest to the smallest—benefit from transformational giving.

A guiding principle that has served nonprofit organizations well is expressed in the philosophy of Martin Buber's *I and Thou:* "All real living is meeting." I paraphrase that statement to read, "All real donor-investors must be met in person by a lay leader from the agency."

Alan L. Wendroff, CFRE
San Francisco, California
October 2000

Acknowledgments

Thanks are in order, of course, to those who helped make this book possible:

To Amy Purvis, who kept things moving in my office while I was exploring the reaches of my experience for the words and ideas that formed my portions of this book;

To Alan L. Wendroff, the "anchor" to my "sail"—whose chapters provide philosophy, strategy, and practical tips that give added dimension to the overall theme and message of the book;

To my clients, colleagues, and workshop attendees who listened as I tried out new ideas on them, and gave me feedback that helped crystallize the ideas in the book;

And to the countless new transformational donors, and those I have come to know, who are partnering with communities and nonprofits around the globe to deliver high impact philanthropy.

KSG

Few books, whether fiction or nonfiction, are written without any help. This book is no exception.

To the very kind and helpful staff and lay leadership of the Goldman Institute on Aging, thank you: Lawrence Z. Feigenbaum, M.D., founder of the Institute; Warren Berl, lay leader extraordinaire; and Judy Loura, director of development.

To Claude N. Rosenberg Jr. and Tim Stone of the Newtithing Group, thank you for giving me complete access to your work.

To Michael J. Franzblau, M.D., the most caring and generous individual I have been privileged to work with in my life as a nonprofit professional.

To my coauthor, Kay Sprinkel Grace, thank you for your kind words and your immense contribution to the literature of the nonprofit sector. You are a pleasure to work with and to be with—never a dull moment with Kay.

To Martha Cooley, who really kept her cool and helped us produce a book that is on target and on point. For the second time, thank you Martha.

ALW

Editor's Introduction

WHAT'S IN THE BOOK

In the Introduction, Kay Sprinkel Grace sets the stage for the book—examining what has been called the "golden age of philanthropy" and calling for nonprofits and investors to work with their communities to ensure the highest impact.

Part I looks at the new philanthropy and its impact on the major gifts culture. Kay Grace begins the book by contrasting the traditional transactional giving and the new transformational giving and presents the community/nonprofit/donor-investor partnership model for high impact philanthropy. The book then goes on to discuss the role of major gifts in the overall development plan, and in that chapter Kay describes major transforming gifts as both a program and a result. Alan Wendroff then lays out the requirements for building a culture within organizations that will support the transformational giving process, followed by Kay's subsequent development the principles and steps needed to make the case for major gifts both inside and outside the organization.

Part II looks at the new donor-investor and Kay explores donor motivation as the key to transformational giving. From there, Alan, looks at the impact of major giving and presents a case study. Chapter 7 carefully reviews the new major donors that are restructuring 21st century philanthropy, and in that chapter Kay cites the opportunities and challenges for organizations and what nonprofits must do to position themselves as sound investments in this new era. Alan expands upon that discussion by looking at specific techniques for research and networking.

Part III develops the new donor/organization partnership. Alan leads off that section with a tactical approach to asking for major gifts and describes new approaches to volunteer and donor involvement. Kay develops new approaches to nonprofit marketing, which is a critical change area in the new philanthropy. In that chapter she uses examples from corporate marketing to emphasize the role values and issues needed to play in non-profit marketing. From there, Kay builds on her earlier writing on stewardship in *Beyond Final Raising*, and applies some new techniques for work with new philanthropists. In the final chapter she covers evaluation: as philanthropy is more and mores results oriented and issue-based, evaluation has grown in importance. This chapter looks at areas and measures of value to all nonprofits.

In the Appendix you will find a management grid for implementing high impact philanthropy in your organization, and a list of additional organizational and bibliographical resources.

EDITOR'S SUMMARY

This book comes at a time when philanthropy is more and more viewed as an increasingly accepted and integral part of a healthy and changing society. We trust this book will provide new ideas and strategies, a broader view of opportunities and some solutions to challenges, and become an indispensable guide for volunteers, donor-investors, and nonprofit and community leaders who wish to put issue-based and values-inspired philanthropy at a new level in their communities through high impact philanthropy.

Martha Cooley
Editor

▼ Introduction

Globally, the twenty-first century has dawned as a golden age for philanthropy. A vibrant level of community investment in the United States has launched a ripple that is being felt worldwide. According to a report from the Boston College Social Welfare Research Institute (SWRI), which measures wealth transfer in three-generation increments, philanthropy will quadruple in the next 50 years. An SWRI report, as summarized in *Success* magazine (July/August 2000), "pegs the transfer of wealth in the United States from 1998 to 2052 at a minimum $41 trillion and as high as $136 trillion." At the same time, according to *Success*, five Internet years have changed the business world, "and that short time has transformed philanthropy as well." In the global village that has become our world, America's philanthropic resources and example have had far-reaching effect, funding programs overseas and stimulating a worldwide interest in and knowledge about philanthropy.

This resurging and robust economy, coupled with an increased understanding by donors of the importance of philanthropy in building stronger communities and institutions, has led to an unprecedented outpouring of generous gifts throughout America and, increasingly, elsewhere in the world. The amount, source, and designation of these gifts vary widely. Their common tie is their impact. This impact is measured in three important ways:

- By the size of the gift relative to the overall budget of the organization or the project
- By the impact of the gift on the social or economic needs and circumstances of the community
- By the impact of the gift on the donor-investor

In each instance, the gift is *transformational*.

Donor-investors who give transformational gifts, organizations that

1

receive them, and communities that benefit from them are forging new and important partnerships. These partnerships increasingly are based on the willingness of each of the partners to adapt to a new age of philanthropy:

- For donor-investors, the willingness to understand the principles and practices of nonprofits and how the ethics, integrity, and values operate to meet human, social, cultural, educational, and other needs of communities
- For nonprofit organizations the willingness to adjust sometimes-creaky bureaucratic systems of decision making, governance, and accountability, and to realize that investors want to see and measure the changes made by their investments as soon as possible
- For communities who benefit from the funding of donor-investors and from the efforts of nonprofits in program and service delivery, the willingness to make a strategic assessment of community needs by identifying *issues,* not just agencies and organizations, so that donor-investors can make a significant impact not just on institutions, but on solving problems

TRANSFORMATIONAL GIVING = HIGH IMPACT PHILANTHROPY

High Impact Philanthropy is about transformational gifts: how nonprofits can attract them, what donor-investors should look for when giving them, how staff and volunteers should steward them, what motivates them, and how to ask for them. *Transformational gifts* may be categorized as big or major gifts, but what distinguishes them is their unique capacity to alter the programs, perceptions, and future of an organization.

Transformational gifts have a measurable impact on the ability of an organization to meet the needs of its constituencies, and each gift represents an investment in the future. Transformational gifts are often given to leverage other gifts, serving as a model and a challenge to other donor-investors. As such, they are not kept quiet, even when they are anonymous.

The concept of transformational giving, defined and developed in Chapter 1, was first applied to large gifts that were given to public universities in the United States by private individuals and foundations. Few in number, but large in impact, these gifts marked a sea change in private support of public institutions. This significant shift—from believing that public higher education was supported by tax dollars alone to realizing that the public institutions of a state were institutions deserving private investment—occurred in the past several decades. As state colleges and universities went from (in the exaggerated description of one dean) "state funded to state assisted to state located," major gifts began transforming these institutions. The idea has now spread to other public and private institutions, including universities in Europe and Asia, and marks a new era and attitude in philanthropy. Transformational gifts are not limited to educational institutions, although they have been the focus of many such gifts.

Our belief in writing this book is that public and private institutions that capably serve their communities through educational, social, health, cultural, and other programs can attract transformational gifts. Because transformational gifts are gauged by their impact on an organization, they range in size; there is no absolute quantitative measure for a gift. Two thousand dollars for a school classroom in inner city Chicago is transforming; so is $250,000 from a foundation to a Boys' and Girls' Club in a small town in Colorado, or $30 million to the Michigan State University. The transformational aspects of these gifts are multiple, and the news about these gifts is widespread.

THE INCREASINGLY PUBLIC FACE OF PHILANTHROPY

Philanthropy in the twenty-first century is front page news. People are talking about large gifts not as isolated or anomalous bursts of individual generosity, but collectively, as a wave that is gathering momentum. It is increasingly apparent that a generation who had been viewed as unaware of their philanthropic responsibilities to community institutions are stepping forward. A study conducted in California's Silicon Valley by the Community Foundation Silicon Valley, as reported by its director, Peter D. Hero, revealed that, "Contrary to common popular perceptions, the reality is that Silicon Valley is remarkably generous. 83% of households in the region give to charity vs. just 69% nationally. Among (our) high net worth households the figure is 94%." The Silicon Valley story is being repeated across America and, increasingly, in countries around the world. The key motivator is investment: From the small foundation in the United Kingdom that invests in a school for the deaf in Nepal, to the massive infusion of funding from major foundations and individual investors in American public education and in global health, people are putting their money into institutions that are addressing the issues of paramount importance to the twenty-first century—and those issues are the business of nonprofits.

Transformational gifts have incredible impact. As a result, organizations want them. Investors want to be sure they will be used wisely, and volunteers want to know how to ask for them and how to steward such gifts once they are received.

Transformational giving is not restricted to those who are the "new philanthropists"—although this book presents ideas about who such people are and what they want. Transformational gifts come from a wide variety of donor-investors, all motivated by the importance of their investments to them, to the organization, and to the community.

UNDERSTANDING URGENCY AND THE TRANSFORMATIONAL GIFT

The twenty-first century has dawned with a diminishing role for governments in creating, preserving, and strengthening community organizations that promote health, welfare, culture, education, and related areas of societal need and interest. The retreat of government funding began in the United States in the 1980s, and has accelerated. In Western Europe, Canada, Asia, and Australia, it has begun more recently. In Asia, Latin America and Africa, private philanthropic investment has gathered speed as governments have failed to keep pace with tremendous social changes and health demands. In Eastern Europe, where fallen governments left little infrastructure behind, private support is also growing. This diminished role for government provides an exciting opportunity for nongovernment, community-based organizations to change the face of their communities by investing in their investors—regarding donors as those who, through these organizations, will help transform our world. The sense of urgency that donors feel about helping to solve problems and address issues of local, regional, national, and global importance is a major impetus to transformational giving. This urgency arises from the sense of well-being and economic stability enjoyed by most developed and some developing nations, and manifests itself in outreach to those whose struggles or opportunities invite support. The Bill and Melinda Gates Foundation, setting the pace with $22 billion in assets, is infusing more than a billion dollars a year into the demanding issues of global health and the improvement of public education. The urgency behind their giving is apparent.

THE TRADITIONAL PHILANTHROPIC PARADIGM HAS SHIFTED

In the accelerated philanthropic environment of the late twentieth and early twenty-first centuries, a paradigm shift occurred—one that has caught many nonprofits by surprise. The shift has been largely inspired by this sense of urgency coupled with a strong identification with issues that tap into donor and community values. Nonprofit organizations, for decades the drivers in the philanthropic sector, now find themselves overtaken by funders who want change to happen more quickly than traditional nonprofit processes allow. They also want a more hands-on role in how their money is managed and spent. These funders view themselves as active investors, not passive donors, selecting their own investment vehicles and monitoring the results much as they would watch the return on investment (ROI) in the stock market. Potential donor-investors seek out those organizations that address the issues they feel are most urgent, reversing the usual process in which nonprofits apply to individuals, foundations, and corporations for funding. Increasing numbers of funders request that organizations not contact them for funds. They identify and seek out those with which they want to become involved.

Nonprofits also find themselves having to be more accountable—a trend that began in the 1970s. They are asked to express their performance in terms of impact and results. Results must be measured in terms investors can understand: how many people served, how many homeless helped, how many children fed, how many young people in the audience, and the cost per person served. Investors want statistics as well as stories. Nonprofits must master the craft of illustrating a statistic (27 foster children placed in permanent homes) with a story that will make the donor remember that every gift has a human dimension (the story of Anna's new family and how she is thriving).

Another change has to do with the way gifts are solicited, and is one that has also been propelled by the impatience of many new donor-investors. The long process traditionally practiced in donor development (identification, qualification, cultivation, etc.) has been challenged by potential donors who want to move more quickly to make an investment that will result in change. Although many potential donors will want to take their time in evaluating an organization and their interest in making a gift, others already know by the time they come to an organization that this is where they want to make their investment. For these individuals, a long process of cultivation is torturous, and they will end up walking away or taking their investment to another organization dealing with the same issue. Just as stewardship is keyed to the interests and needs of the donor (Grace, 1997), organizations must adapt their systems and practices to cultivate and solicit the needs of their investors.

Another major aspect of this paradigm shift is that the process for implementing change within nonprofits seems too cumbersome to many. In a fast-paced dot.com world, nonprofit structures can seem very outdated. Too often governed by processes that have not been evaluated in years, nonprofits lag in the speed with which they launch programs. Attempts to work with and within nonprofits are frustrating to those who want to make an impact immediately, and many nonprofits, unable to adjust their processes to the needs of donors, find themselves standing by while donors create and implement their own organizations and strategies for making an impact on their communities.

The number of smaller family and community foundations in America doubled from 22,000 to 44,000 between 1980 and 1998, with much of that growth occurring in the 1990s. (*Success* magazine, July/August 2000, p. 34). Community foundations, particularly those in the fastest growing wealth centers in the United States, were deluged by newly wealthy individuals (whether from inheritance, stock options, or the formation or sale of a company) wanting to establish donor advised funds. Many of these donor-advised funds have become operating foundations, providing programming as well as funding.

A key purpose of this book is to help nonprofits adapt their systems and structures to meet the needs of donor-investors who have a sense of urgency about the issues and values in which they believe. It is designed to help those nonprofits be more aware, responsive and accountable.

PARTNERS IN TRANSFORMING COMMUNITIES: THE NONPROFIT AND THE DONOR-INVESTOR

This book is not just for nonprofit organizations and their staffs, boards, and other volunteers. It is also for donor-investors who want to make a difference, who want to become more involved in the issues and the impact that are intrinsic to transformational philanthropy.

Donor-investors survey the nonprofit sector and see over a million nonprofits in the United States and an increasing number abroad. Those with whom we spoke—and those surveyed increasingly by public organizations interested in the field of philanthropy—confess their confusion about where to invest their money, what happens to their money when they invest it, and exactly how they can become involved with the organizations they fund. This book provides examples and insights for the donor-investor, while offering nonprofit performance guidelines that can become the investment standard for donors. The creation of new nonprofits or organizations addressing community issues may be necessary, but it should not be done before the avenues for creating partnerships with existing institutions have been explored.

These are times of tremendous opportunity for nonprofits and their donor-investors and communities. To capitalize on these opportunities, those who desire transformational gifts, and those who would give them, need to understand the paradigm shifts that have occurred in major giving. It is that review with which we begin this book, providing the foundation for what follows.

THE NEW PHILANTHROPY AND ITS IMPACT ON THE MAJOR GIFTS CULTURE

1 ▼ The New Organization

Redefining Major Gifts

High impact philanthropy is based on the belief that communities, nonprofits, and donor-investors increasingly are partners in the strengthening of communities in America and around the world. Communities that benefit from these partnerships go beyond geography: They include those who cluster locally, regionally, nationally, or globally around an issue, problem, or idea.

The catalyst for high impact philanthropy is transformational giving.

Each member plays a unique role in the high impact philanthropy partnership, and all members are essential.

- Communities provide the vision, needs assessments, and trend analyses that allow nonprofits to address both the urgent and important issues
- Nonprofits provide vision, staffing, expertise, networks, and client services
- Donor-investors provide the financial resources and strategic involvement to ensure delivery of programs that will meet community needs.

The simplicity of this partnership belies its potential: If the partnership can function effectively and consistently in communities around the world, then this new golden age of philanthropy will have the promised impact.

Expectations for the impact of philanthropy in the twenty-first century are high. To meet them, all the partners must fulfill their roles:

- Communities need to identify their needs in a more cohesive and consistent way, and convey those needs as opportunities for partnership with nonprofits and investors.
- Nonprofit organizations need to change the way they view, approach, solicit, and steward major gifts. Nonprofits must shift from an institutional focus to an issues, constituency, and donor-investor focus.

EXHIBIT 1.1 The High Impact Philanthropy Model: Balanced Partnerships for Issues-Based Philanthropy

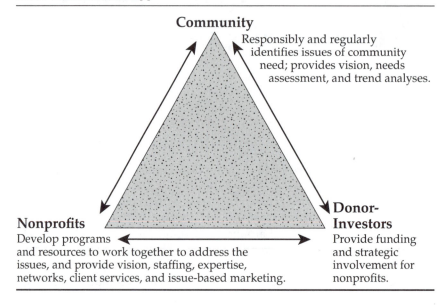

Community
Responsibly and regularly identifies issues of community need; provides vision, needs assessment, and trend analyses.

Nonprofits
Develop programs and resources to work together to address the issues, and provide vision, staffing, expertise, networks, client services, and issue-based marketing.

Donor-Investors
Provide funding and strategic involvement for nonprofits.

- Donor-investors need to be informed about the opportunities for investment that exist in communities and educated in the ways of philanthropy so they can make discerning choices among the organizations that address the issues, ideas, and problems about which donor-investors are concerned.

WHY THE NONPROFIT'S APPROACH TO MAJOR GIVING NEEDS TO CHANGE

The proliferation of nonprofits has increased the number of choices donor-investors can make about where their money is invested in the community. The competition is stiff, and the ability of nonprofits to position themselves successfully for major gifts requires a much greater focus, both on the donor-investor and on the community issues or needs the organization is meeting. To be successful, organizations must identify their values and issues, convey them actively in the community, and base their major donor outreach and involvement efforts on those values and issues.

The bottom line is that increasing numbers of major donors are looking for more satisfaction than just helping nonprofits reach their financial goals. They are looking for tangible evidence that their gifts are making a difference, and they want to know from the outset what the potential impact is. They are also looking for involvement for themselves and for accountability from the organization.

It is not only among the newer philanthropists that these phenomena are apparent. One donor, a long-time supporter of a particular issue through several agencies that she supports, has grown increasingly impatient with the passive stewardship and lack of accountability provided by several of the organizations she has always supported, she is now focusing more of her giving on another organization—one that deals with the same issue, but that has given her a more active role in providing advice and counsel. She feels the organization's interest is sincere and that its staff members listen to her. She feels respected not only for her financial support but for her ideas and experience as well.

TODAY'S MAJOR DONORS: CREATING NEW MODELS FOR PHILANTHROPIC GIVING

Another influential aspect of twenty-first century philanthropy is the number of donors who want to choose the organization to which they will give. They want to identify those organizations whose missions reflect issues of importance to them, whose values support theirs, and whose management is sound. This presents a challenge for nonprofits used to initiating the process themselves—identifying potential major funders, conducting research, initiating cultivation, preparing proposals, arranging site visits, and then waiting for the response. Now, there is a new way of doing business. Nonprofits must learn to position themselves effectively through marketing and public relations and through consistency in messages, based not only on their merits as organizations but on the way in which they are helping to solve issues of common community concern.

The growth of family foundations among those with newly earned or inherited wealth is one of the major early trends in twenty-first-century philanthropy. Often the role of the board members of these family foundations is the active pursuit of appropriate organizations to fund. In the past, some family foundations were created because the families had certain organizations they wanted to fund and this was the most appropriate way to focus that giving. Today, the newer family foundations are very issue-focused. They also tend to involve younger members of the family. One foundation, established in the late 1990s, involves the teenage children in the decision making, and lets them practice their philanthropy by designating gifts to areas of special interest to them.

It is not unusual for the representatives of these new foundations to request a meeting with someone from an organization the family is researching—to test whether the organization meets *their* criteria for investment relative to the issues they feel are important. A great deal hinges on the response by the nonprofit to that initial contact by the foundation: The organization's response will be evaluated for its timeliness, quality, and preparation, and as an indicator of the viability of a potential investor relationship. A sluggish response or a poorly prepared meeting—or worse, an arrogance on the part of a nonprofit that it is "the only game in town"—may doom that nonprofit's chances for funding. As a sector, we need to realize that, with a whole new wave of vibrant and interested funders, we need to change the way we do business.

TRANSACTIONAL VERSUS TRANSFORMATIONAL GIFTS

It is time to look at major gifts with a fresh perspective, one that will ensure the continued involvement of the donor-investor, the repeated support of these donor-investors, in varying forms, including additional major gifts, regular annual gifts, and planned gifts, and the ability of the organization to continue to meet its mission and the needs it has identified, and to serve its community.

In traditional major giving, the emphasis was on the *transaction*. It was an internally driven process with the donor as the outside part of the equation. To meet ambitious goals, major gifts officers were instructed to focus on the transaction, and the activities leading up to it, and the best major gifts officers were experts in these transactions. This focus on the transaction, rather than on the values exchange, mission link, and potential impact of the gift on both the donor and the institution, diminished the opportunities for donor connection and stewardship that would lead to long-term relationships and repeated gifts. Major gifts programs slipped into a routine—goal-focused rather than outcome-focused—that led, in far too many cases, to the decline of the overall major gifts program at a time when

EXHIBIT 1.2 Transactional Giving as The Bell Curve

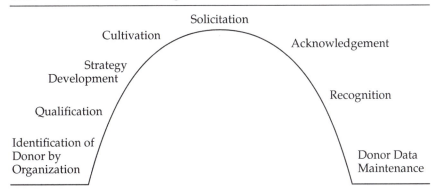

In this model, the curve begins again when a new gift is needed, and the cycle, with previous donors, begins with qualification and follows the same curve.

it should have been on the increase. This was particularly true at what is often called the *special gifts* level: those gifts that usually fall just under the official designation for major gifts in large institutions, or those gifts that in smaller institutions may be for special projects and not really fall into the annual budget or merit a special campaign. Many potentially major and long-term donor-investors were lost from programs like these because of the transactional focus. Their giving needed to be viewed relative to its impact: from that basis, a relationship is easily developed.

In transformational giving, the focus is on the impact of the gift and the renewing relationship, not just on the transaction. Although the transaction should be geared to the needs, style, and wishes of the donor within the scope and mission of the organization, the focus must be on the transforming nature of the gift.

Defining Transformational Gifts

Transformational gifts are voluntary contributions from individuals, foundations, or corporations to nonprofit organizations, the size and focus of which initiate and often sustain significant transformation or change in the organization, in the donor, and even in the community. These contributions may be categorized as "big" or "major" gifts, but their unique capacity to alter the programs, perception, and future of an organization distinguish

EXHIBIT 1.3 Transformational Giving as an Infinity Loop

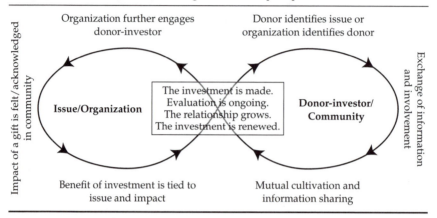

them from other big or major gifts. More than gifts, they are true investments in the future of an organization and of the community. Transformational giving goes beyond the donor's usual annual transactional gift. Transformational gifts are an inclusive investment of the donor's values made in organizations whose values the donor shares. The resultant values exchange results in high impact philanthropy.

MAJOR GIFTS, FROM TRANSACTIONAL TO TRANSFORMATIONAL: SOME OF THE BASICS REMAIN

Major gifts have traditionally constituted the upper end of the gift pyramid, and they still do. These basic aspects remain true of major gifts:

- They are categorized as major based on the relationship of the amount to the size of the organization's annual budget or to a capital or endowment campaign goal.
- Major gifts can be unrestricted (for use wherever the need is greatest) or restricted to a particular program, person, or purpose. There are recurring major restricted gifts (e.g., for learning disability programs, scholarship support, free breast cancer screenings, dance touring, curator acquisition funds, etc.), although most major annual gifts are unre-

stricted. Conversely, there are nonrecurring, unrestricted major gifts (e.g., an undesignated bequest, or a campaign gift for unrestricted program support).

- There are recurring major gifts and nonrecurring major gifts (e.g., campaign, endowment, or planned gifts). A *recurring* major gift is one that is given annually or often enough that it can be counted on; a *nonrecurring* major gift is one that will not be repeated again (or in some cases, not for a very long time). The following quadrant, developed by Linda Moerschbaecher, a San Francisco planned-giving attorney, shows how these gifts can be "mixed and matched" in a well-developed major gifts program:

Restricted	Unrestricted
Nonrecurring	Recurring

All major transformational gifts still fit into this quadrant. Connecting any of the boxes vertically or diagonally to another describes all the ways in which major gifts can be given.

TRADITIONAL APPROACHES TO MAJOR GIFTS: INTERNAL GOAL SETTING AND COMMON PRACTICES

Most institutions, whether large (universities, established independent boarding and day schools, hospitals, religious organizations, national health organizations, major cultural institutions) or small (independent day schools, community museums, local clinics), have traditionally set a major gifts goal each year. This goal is usually a percentage of a fund-raising budget figure that is based on the total amount that must be raised to meet the budget, rather than on a careful consideration of the ways in which those gifts could have a deeper and lasting impact on the institution, the community, the institution's constituency, and the donor.

Although these desired gifts are usually pegged to a case for support, the case is most often defined in terms of organizational needs (computers, beds, playgrounds, unrestricted current program support) than in terms of the needs the organization is trying to meet in the community (*why* the computers, beds, playgrounds, and program support are needed). Goals are usually derived from planning processes that are the result of looking in mirrors at institutional needs rather than through windows at the community. Too little market analysis is done and zero-based program planning and budgeting is viewed by too many organizations as a threat. Organizations find themselves seeking major gifts for programs or services that may no longer be meeting community needs. Worse, sometimes money is raised for projects that never happen, or are never completed, and donor accountability is poor. Large organizations, and smaller organizations with less complexity or experienced staffing in their fund development, will plug in an arbitrary figure to raise from major donors in their annual funds.

When the money is fixed to institutional needs, the appeal for gifts is based on an internally-motivated goal. Targets are derived from how much money is needed to meet a goal rather than from defined community needs and the existence of prospects who can and will make those gifts. Too often, potential donors with no relationship to the organization are assigned to major gifts officers who, for their own employment evaluations, have ambitious fund-raising goals to achieve. This pressure leads to a transactional approach based more on the accumulation of gifts to reach an internal goal than on the development of relationships with investors. More than one major gifts officer has expressed the exhaustion of always trying to raise more and more, without a reward system in place that recognizes ongoing relationships with existing donors. They feel as though they are making cold calls.

VOLUNTEER ROLE IN TRADITIONAL MAJOR GIVING PROGRAMS

An unfortunate trend that began in the late twentieth century, particularly among large institutions with full major gifts staffs, was the increased reliance on staff people to initiate, cultivate, solicit, and steward major gifts without the partnership of volunteers. The decline in the number of volunteers involved in fund-raising at many major universities and other institutions is a curious trend, one that hopefully will not continue.

A strong major gifts program attribute has been, and continues to be, the involvement of volunteers as partners in the development process. The subject of countless training sessions and meetings, the growth of board members and other volunteers into comfortable askers was and is a tremendous benefit of the transactional approach. Viewed correctly as a critical part of the transaction because of their links to the prospects and existing donors, volunteers have been a force in increasing the leverage power of most successful major gifts programs. Volunteer linkage is vital, and is the principal reason for involving volunteers in the major gifts process—but there is another reason for involving them as well: The more they exercise their roles as asker-advocates, the more committed they become to the mission. Their enthusiasm for their roles as ambassadors and capable spokespeople increases, and they become more effective in all aspects of the organization's governance, programs, and outreach efforts. They become effective agents in transformational giving as the stewards of relationships.

TRADITIONAL SOURCES OF MAJOR GIFTS

Major or transformational gifts in start-up organizations, unless the organization was seed funded by one or more individual donors, traditionally came from foundation funding. Reliance on foundations was seen as short-term while other sources of funding were being developed from individuals, associations, corporations, or government. Some organizations were successful at weaning themselves from heavy foundation support and involving new sources of funding; others were not. In general, major gifts—particularly those publicly recognized as transformational—remained the success stories of larger cultural, educational, health, or other institutions or of highly experienced smaller organizations with an urgent mission to fulfill.

OTHER PRACTICES THAT CHARACTERIZE TRANSACTIONAL GIVING PROGRAMS

One persistent practice of smaller (and some larger) organizations—a practice that defies everything we are learning about the donor as an investor—was that of not going back to a major donor in the following year to ask for another gift. When asked why a particular donor was not solicited again, the organization would reply that it did not want the donor to think it needed the money. This stance led to two destructive outcomes: (1) The donor was neither involved as an investor nor given an opportunity to reinvest in a program that was fulfilling both the donor's and the organization's dream for the community; and (2) the organization found itself frantically searching every year (or every campaign) for new major donors. The only valid reason for not asking in subsequent years or campaigns is that the donor has said not to. Otherwise, it is poor stewardship *not* to go back to donors for additional support for programs in which they have become investors. The concern about being perceived as needing more money is groundless in the donor-investor and transformational giving models. When a person invests in a nonprofit and is satisfied with the impact of that investment, he or she will *want* to make additional investments. It is a way of enhancing the original investment and ensuring the continued delivery on mission by the organization. The donor feels ownership for the success of the program and wants to stay involved.

Another practice that fit with transactional programs but does not belong in transformational programs relates to donor involvement. In more traditional major giving, donors typically were not involved and, in too many cases for comfort, did not even receive adequate communication relative to the impact of the gift on the mission and the community. One donor who gave an impact-level gift of $7,000 to a tiny organization in her community never heard from the organization again. It is still in existence, but she has not given again.

In traditional major giving, the philanthropy that was encouraged, and that resulted, was more passive than active. Today's newer philanthropists refer to this as "checkbook philanthropy." Donors gave, they were thanked, and they were then left alone (unless they were board members or involved in an advisory capacity) with only occasional communication until it was time to be asked again. Assumptions were too frequently made that donors did not want to be involved, they just wanted to give. In fact, organizations somehow assumed that donors would not want to be bothered. We now realize that many of these donors were never asked if they wanted to be involved, and many would have become involved if asked. To be effective partners with donor-investors and communities, nonprofits will need to shift from transactional giving to transformational giving.

EIGHT COMMON ASPECTS OF MAJOR TRANSFORMATIONAL GIFTS

While the size of the gift is still the aspect on which we focus, there are eight other aspects common to all major transformational gifts, regardless of their size.

1. Transformational gifts have an impact on the organization, its constituency, the donor, and the community.
2. A gift's designation as transformational often has much to do with how it is cultivated, solicited, and stewarded.
3. Transformational gifts are more than gifts; they are investments (Grace, 1997).
4. Gifts are motivated by shared values between the investor and the organization.
5. Gifts are rooted in a belief in the importance of the organization's mission, and increasingly, they are issue driven.
6. Donor-investors expect solid return from two bottom lines: the return on values, and the management of their investment.
7. Just as a gift is designated major by its size relative to the budget or the campaign goal, some donor-investors should be treated like major donors because of the relationship of the size of their gift to their capacity to give.
8. An organization does not have to be large or long established to attract a major gift, as long as the mission or issue is big in the eyes (or heart) of the donor.

Examining the Eight Aspects of the Major Transformational Gift

1. Transformational gifts have an impact on the organization, its constituency, the donor, and on the community. This is the most important qualifier for a major transforming gift, because it determines the way in which the organization stewards both the gift and the giver. The notion of *impact* is one that brings into consideration not just the organization, but its mission in the community. A gift that establishes, for example, an endowed book fund for a library, a choreographer's fund for a dance company, a scholarship fund for a school or college, a particular collection or program for a museum, or a physician's position in a clinic in an under-served area of a community, cannot be measured by the impact on the budget alone. Such a gift must be measured, recognized, honored, and respected for its impact on the community members whose needs the organization is meeting: those who use the library, the choreographers whose artistry will affect both dancers and audiences, the people who will visit and be educated by the collection or program, the young people or adult students who will have access to education, and the people who will be served by the clinic in the community. These are the true measurements of impact—and the best test of a transforming major gift. In soliciting major gifts it is essential to focus on the benefits to the community of such an investment. Too often, the focus is put instead on the benefit to the *organization*. Although it is, indeed, the organization that delivers the program that has the impact, the ultimate measure of a gift is the impact itself. Philanthropy (Payton, 1988) has one or both of two purposes: to ease human suffering, and/or to enhance human potential. Organizations should not forget those measures when cultivating, soliciting, and stewarding major gifts.

The initial gift of $15 million to the San Francisco Asian Art Museum from Chong Moon Lee, a Korean-American businessman, transformed the community perception of the museum's $160 million capital campaign, and also provided much-needed leverage for attracting other transactional gifts. The involvement of this donor since the gift was made has exceeded his involvement before the gift was made, and has led to further investment on his part and to his willingness to be involved in the solicitation of other transforming gifts.

2. *A gift's designation as transformational often has much to do with how it is cultivated, solicited, and stewarded.* As described earlier in this chapter, transactional giving focuses on the transaction itself: Systematic cultivation and appropriate solicitation lead to a gift. The gift is negotiated with the donor, properly acknowledged, and then put to work in the organization and for the community. After the receipt of the gift, the appropriate recognition for the gift (plaque, reception, dinner) is seen as the end of the transaction. If the donor is already involved as a current or former board member, then there will be continued (but not necessarily increased) involvement.

Transformational gifts, should be viewed as the beginning of a new relationship. Focus shifts to the way in which the gift, or investment, *transforms* the organization, the people the organization serves, the community and the donor. This shift leads, ultimately, to a partnership with the donor, one that goes back to the roots of philanthropy identified by de Toqueville (*Democracy in America*, 1831): the need people have to make a difference. The spread of America's approach to philanthropy to the rest of the world has been slower than other aspects, but the movement is underway. Philanthropy throughout the world is changing, principally the aspect of the relationship with the donor. The donor-investor's connection with the organization, in transformational giving, must be maintained through identification and involvement with the program, not just with the administration. Always a motivation, donors today are more outspoken about wanting to be connected with the program (artistic director, counselor, curator, holder of the chair funded by the donor). Organizations need to create ongoing opportunities for donor-investors and potential donor-investors to connect often with program. Having a mission message at each board meeting is a strong component in maintaining board-member focus on program, but most organizations do not provide that same opportunity for donor-investors who are not on the board. A donor becomes a donor-investor (Grace, 1997), and the gift becomes the catalyst for involving the donor-investor in the impact of the gift. Communication about impact relies on program staff and on the people who directly benefit from the gift.

3. Transformational gifts are more than gifts: they are investments (Grace, 1997). Increasingly, those who give large gifts and are interviewed by the press speak of their gifts not as donations or contributions but as investments. These are savvy people who understand the leveraging power of making an investment in an idea or issue of importance to the community. The landscape of philanthropy is changing so fast that organizations need to shift their attitudes toward gifts and givers to acknowledge that these are now investments and investors. These investors expect the values and financial-stability return on the information provided, they expect consistent and accurate information, they expect to be invited to become involved (even if they choose not to), and they expect interaction with the people in the organization who are delivering the programs, not just with administrators. They also expect a certain amount of access to those programs. Executive directors are learning to live with new paradigms in staff-board, staff-nonboard volunteer, and staff-investor relationships.

4. Gifts are motivated by shared values by the investor and the organization. Philanthropy is the way people act on the values they share with an organization, and on the values they hold dear for their lives, their families and their communities (Grace, 1997). Promoting these values is paramount in positioning nonprofits for significant transformational gifts. Nonprofits chronically shy away from openness about their values, fearing that potential donors will think they are emotional or inappropriate. When nonprofits began to respond to the growing need for accountability in the 1980s, they adopted (appropriately) more corporate management and reporting systems. Along with this positive step, however, nonprofits took a companion action that in retrospect was ill-advised. In adopting more corporate mission statements, many organizations forgot that nonprofit mission statements must incorporate the *why* (the values) of their existence. Mission statements focused only on *what* the organization did or was doing, which was descriptive, but not inspiring. In a message-driven world in which product and service commercials based entirely on values are commonplace, the nonprofit marketplace has chosen to submerge its values in its quest to appear more corporate. This misses the point. Nonprofits need to be managed and evaluated as responsible businesses, but the attraction for donors is still going to be the issue at hand: a human or societal issue of primary importance to the shared values by the community and the potential donor.

5. Gifts are rooted in a belief in the importance of the organization's mission, and increasingly, they are issue driven.   Increasingly, gifts are issue driven, and the mission statement needs to express those issues, not simply describe the organization. A mission statement that describes what the organization does may not describe the issue (homelessness, access to art or culture for all citizens, education with and about diversity, etc.) in a way that attracts the attention of people interested in funding that issue. Traditional philanthropic approaches have been based on attracting donors to fund an *organization.* Now, although that is the ultimate goal, funders want to first find out what your *issue* is, whether it matches with their interests, and whether this would be a good investment. Every communications piece from an organization should focus on quantifying and describing the need or issue, why it is important to the community, and what the organization is doing about it. It should contain some examples of specific individuals or groups who have benefited from the work of the organization in addressing this issue, and should indicate who is already involved and how others can become engaged. Brochures and press releases that continue to focus only on the organization and its needs are not inspiring to donors. They do not deal with the issues that allow a community to come together around shared beliefs and values—and increasingly, they do not attract significant gifts. The $100 million gift in 1999 to the University of Mississippi was given by an alumnus, but its purpose was to address the chronic issue of illiteracy in the state of Mississippi. The donors are concerned about the *issue;* they have identified University of Mississippi as the agency to address that issue in their home state.

6. Donor-investors expect solid return from two bottom lines: the return on values, and the demonstration of sound financial practices.   Accountability is here to stay. This important nonprofit achievement of the late twentieth century helped position the sector as the appropriate vehicle to take up where government had left off, and to do it better. It happened first in the United States and is now happening throughout much of the world. From Bangkok to Berlin, from Paris to Pittsburgh, from Milwaukee to Memphis, organizations are turning increasingly to the private sector for support as government funding recedes and/or as government programs reveal themselves to be inappropriate to provide a particular program or service efficiently. However, in the nonprofit's heightened focus on the financial bottom line, it is important to remember the other bottom line: the *return on values* (Grace, 1997). A great deal of the donor's values are imbedded in the gift, particularly with transformational gifts. With values investment comes expectations—not only for financial performance, but also for clear reporting on the values that are being upheld and enhanced. Annual reporting needs to be numbers-strong and values-clear. Excellent annual reports are rich with photographs and stories that make clear the connection between financial investment and values return.

7. Just as a gift is designated major by its size relative to the budget or the campaign goal, some donor-investors should be treated like major donors because of the relationship of the size of their gift to their capacity to give. Transformational giving differs from transactional giving in that it is not formulaic. Although the internal benchmarks for major gifts are still maintained, particularly as they relate to general recognition practices, the emphasis on relationships and involvement in transformational giving allows organizations to involve and appreciate those donors whose gifts may not be at the benchmark level on an absolute scale, but whose gifts relative to their ability to give make them truly transformational in its effect on them as donors. Furthermore, the transformational nature of these gifts extends to the inspiration their donors provide to board members and other volunteers, to staff, and to other potential donor-investors. Their stories generate interest and commitment in others. One National Society of Fund-Raising Executives (NSFRE) chapter selected a donor like this as its Philanthropist of the Year. Her total giving was, over her lifetime, much less than other philanthropists might give in a year; but as a person who had worked all her life as a domestic servant and had given everything she could into a scholarship fund for students who otherwise would not have a chance at a better life, she had helped transform the community.

8. An organization does not have to be large or long established to attract a major gift, as long as the mission is big in the eyes (or heart) of the donor. Although large established institutions are most apt to receive truly transforming gifts, a growing number of smaller organizations—particularly those addressing critical educational, social, health, and cultural issues in our communities—find themselves singled out by issues-focused philanthropists for transformational gifts. A chamber music orchestra with a budget of less than a half million dollars received three annual $100,000 gifts in a row from an individual who does not accept solicitations: He chooses which organizations he funds. Similarly, another small orchestra receives regular support for its recording program from an individual who chooses to remain anonymous. This person's support has allowed the discography of the orchestra to achieve a remarkable level of productivity and quality. The key point is the importance of the mission, not the size of the organization. It has been standard practice in more traditional philanthropy that smaller and/or newer organizations felt they had to wait before they could solicit really large gifts. In twenty-first-century philanthropy, the options for all organizations depend on three key factors that are not pegged to size or age:

- the importance of the need the organization is meeting
- the way the issue is marketed to the community
- and the success of the organization's planned or actual approach to the issue.

CONCLUSION

These eight aspects of major transformational gifts form the foundation of this book. In nonprofits of all sizes, major gifts are both a goal and a program. Aspired to by small organizations, and mastered by large organizations, major gifts are the fulcrum of successful development operations. They are a critical part of institutional stability—strengthening programs, building endowment, creating operating or capital reserves that guarantee the continuity of services, and signaling to the community that the organization is capable of attracting and managing significant philanthropic investment.

The Role of Major Gifts in the Overall Development Plan

Enhancing the Mission

Major giving, long regarded as the end product of a serial progression through the various stages of annual contributions, is changing. More and more, it is seen as the ultimate investment in mission. Spurred by donor impatience, the urgency of mission-related needs in the community, and a greater awareness of the nonprofit/donor-investor/community partnership in strengthening society, fresh and creative approaches to the major or transformational giving process are not only possible, they are imperative.

Organizations find themselves increasingly able to leverage major transformational gifts from donors who may not have established a giving pattern with the nonprofit. As noted in chapter 1 (later developed in chapter 8), this is because of donors' *issues* focus: Some of today's major donors are so drawn to issues that they are willing to make a major investment in an organization with which they've had no previous relationship, as long as the organization demonstrates it can effectively address its mission: health, social, cultural, religious, or other community needs.

To manage a mission-fulfilling transformational giving program effectively, one must regard major gifts in two ways. Whether a donor progresses gradually through various steps on the development ladder, or whether he or she enters into a relationship with the nonprofit by making an initial transformational gift, the major gifts efforts of an organization toward the donor are both a *program* (it must be well organized) and a *re-*

sult (of cultivation, relationship building, shared values and effective solicitation).

APPROACHING MAJOR GIFTS AS A PROGRAM

There must be basic organization within the development or administrative department of an organization to sustain a major gifts effort and attract transformational givers. Although an occasional gift will come in without a direct request, and although some of an organization's most faithful donors will be patient with slow acknowledgement or inaccurate tracking of their gifts, most others will not. Particularly dissatisfied will be the younger or newer philanthropists who are used to the benefits and efficiencies of well-constructed and-maintained databases in their workplaces and homes. They are highly intolerant of seemingly amateur or disorganized procedures that call themselves "systems" but are not. In creating a program, the following basic organizational elements must be present.

A Clearly Stated Mission Focused on Issues, Not on the Institution

This is critical. If an organization cannot express itself in terms of the needs and issues it addresses, rather than in terms of the needs it has as an organization, then it will not be as well positioned to attract and maintain major transformational gifts. If you want to be competitive, dust off your mission statement. Get professional help in writing it if necessary. Take a look at your materials. In chapter 10, the concept of marketing with and for impact is developed and some examples are given. Nonprofits that master the language of development marketing can see great results. Sage Hill School, a new independent high school in Orange County whose values-based development is recounted in chapter 4, settled on a powerful marketing theme for its recruitment and outreach: "The tradition begins with you." Our sector can learn from the for-profit sector, which has mastered the art of incorporating values language into intriguing marketing pieces. We see it every day in the media; chapter 10 provides some provocative examples. Because our values focus is the basis of our existence as a sector, our mission statements should reflect them.

Commitment by the Board, Other Volunteers, Staff Leadership, and Program Staff

People must be committed to the effort required and to the benefits to be derived from developing a strong, mission-based major gifts program, and from putting the program to work. Transformational gifts require a commitment by the entire organization, at an appropriate, and sometimes changing, level of involvement.

- *For board and administrative leadership,* a commitment to develop and approve a budget that will support not only fund-raising (dollars spent relative to dollars received with direct mail, telephone, special events) but also development (cultivation, stewardship, long-term relationship building, enhanced communication tools).
- *For all leadership,* the knowledge and understanding that major transformational gifts are the future of the organization, and that they will require the organization to make an investment that may not have immediate return. This is particularly true for organizations whose communications materials and programs may reflect an organization-focused mission or a lack of development marketing focus.
- *For program staff,* who are essential to transformational giving, willingness to become involved with the major gifts program when they are called on to participate in tours and meetings, to allow visits to their programs by potential donors (if appropriate) and to prepare proposals and budgets when requested. Because most nonprofits work their program staffs pretty hard within the scope of their normal job descriptions, the benefits of participation in a major gifts program may have to be sold.

    A word to the wise: If some program staff are resistant and resentful, work initially with those whose acceptance of the process is more likely. Identify those on staff who are willing to be involved, and hope that their enthusiasm will eventually convince others. At a major public university, the faculty of one of the colleges was particularly antagonistic about the dean's requests that they get involved with major gift development. In frustration, the dean finally identified one professor who was already cultivating a potential major donor, and worked with him. They brought in a transformational gift to the professor's program and the impact of that gift was so great that the dean found herself with a much more willing faculty. They had a leader from their own ranks as a cheerleader for the major gifts program, emphasizing the fun he had working with the donor and asking for the gift.

    Finally, but of primary importance, is the need to make sure that the appropriate development staff are in place to manage a growing major gifts program; this imperative will be addressed later in this chapter.

A Computerized Donor-Tracking System

An off-the-shelf product is preferable for most organizations. Custom products carry with them the danger that those who built them will not be there to service or upgrade them, and that the basic system will be incompatible with accounting or other companion databases within the organization. Capacity should be appropriate to future, not just current, aspirations. The system should grow with the organization. Although programs vary, a solid system will have an adequate field for tracking names, addresses, gifts, and contacts, a comment field that tolerates complete sentences, and other information that formats to a standard report. Be sure to evaluate the reports before you sign on to buy a system. Make sure you can access the information you need about prospects, current and lapsed donors, and others on your mailing list.

MAJOR GIFTS AS PART OF A CONTINUUM

Although it is important to have a major gifts program in an organization, there is a danger in compartmentalizing major gifts to the extent that the program pulls away from the annual giving program or the planned giving program. Instead, you should view major gifts as an overlay onto these two distinct areas of giving.

In many organizations with complex and mature development programs, major gifts and planned gifts are combined into one single effort, called *major gift planning.* This designation recognizes that people who are capable of making a large transforming gift to an organization may make it outright, or they may choose some form of planned gift. The key concept in this model is developing a *continuum* of opportunities that are both well defined and keyed to donor motivations. The annual giving program is part of that continuum. Annual major gifts may not be transforming in themselves, but the aggregate of these gifts can often transform a particular program or an entire organization from one that struggles from year to year to one with a secure base of funding.

Organizing a Major Gifts Program

Development-office leadership shines in the organization of a major gifts program. Small organizations need not feel as though they cannot position themselves for major gifts. The measure of an organization is not its size, but the importance of its mission. Developing a major gifts category among annual gifts is very important, as is attracting the transforming gifts that are seed or continuation money for programs. In mission-based development, nonprofits are able to focus on the needs they are meeting and to position their resulting resource requirements as opportunities for major investors to make a difference. If the need is so large that it will require a doubling of the organization's budget over the next several years, then even the smallest organization can make the case for investment to a prospective donor. However, in making the case, the organization must fortify its position by having a well organized approach to cultivating, soliciting, and managing major or transforming investments.

A number of key ingredients are needed for the successful development of a regular stream of major or transforming gifts. These are discussed in the following pages.

1. Make the case internally. Having the interest and cooperation of program staff will make major gift fund-raising much easier. Although we count on executive and development staff to organize the actual investment, it is the program staff that most effectively positions the importance of making the investment. Orchestras, for example, need the full cooperation of the music director or conductor. He or she must be available to meet with potential donors, be willing to have interested potential investors at open rehearsals, and to describe passionately and accurately why the orchestra is worthy of significant investment. Similarly, the program director for a homeless shelter, the counselor at a camp for disabled adults, the head of an independent school, and the occupational therapist at a center for handicapped children all need to feel comfortable with their roles in the cultivation of major gifts. In some cases, these individuals are willing to make the actual ask; in most cases, they are not. However, their role prior to the ask is what makes the ask possible, particularly if a funding proposal is required. They may be called upon to supply the information, to write the proposal, or to edit a proposal written by another staff member. The internal marketing of the benefits of participating in major gifts activities must be the first step. Without the enthusiasm of program staff, the major gifts program loses passion and credibility. This point, and the next, are developed more fully in chapter 4.

2. Make the case externally with materials that are appropriate to the organization and its mission.   The development of materials to support major gifts outreach is increasingly a tailoring proposition. Except in major capital campaigns for large institutions, nonprofits have veered away from expensive, four-color glossy printed materials, and toward flexible desktop-published print materials often supplemented by a videotape or other visual resources.

A further issue relative to materials is that donors should not be given the impression that too much has been spent. This is particularly true for small organizations that are addressing big issues. The San Francisco Food Bank, in its successful $5 million campaign for a new building, was very prudent not only in the cost and appearance of its eventual printed materials but also in conveying one of its strongest case points: the low percentage of overhead relative to program investment. Several of the key donors and volunteers repeatedly commented that they were drawn to the food bank because of its overall fiscal management and the image that it conveyed to other donors. Recognizing the different values and interests of potential donors and the sensitivity of some to the production of seemingly costly materials, the wise organization avoids one-size-fits-all materials that require a great deal of focused retrofitting. The flexible approach has a number of advantages: donor focus, cost savings, the ability to update frequently, and the fact that it sends a fiscally prudent message to the potential donor.

In major gift fund raising, the emphasis is less on the materials and more on securing the connection and investment through personal involvement. Many mega-gifts have been successfully solicited without benefit of printed materials. One capital campaign secured a gift of $1 million from a community foundation through a combination of personal communication, a four-page letter proposal that reflected those personal conversations, and an eight-minute video that provided an overview of the organization's impact in the community. In other cases, no written materials were provided. Instead, the donor looked at drawings of a proposed building or met with program staff who eagerly described how an investment would change lives by strengthening programs and services. The increased use of web sites also has an impact on potential investors. A $100,000 gift to a community foundation came after the donor read the foundation's web site. One performing arts center, during construction, updated its web site with ever-expanding photographs of the building. This persuaded at least one potential major donor, who had been cultivated extensively by the organization, that the project was really going to happen and that it was a good investment. Conversely, if commitment to keep the web site updated is lacking, it is a poor place for potential major donors to go. To visit a site in September and find that it has not been updated since June conveys a negative message about the overall organization. Organizations that put up a web site need to invest in a web master who will keep the site updated.

3. Involve volunteers as leaders and solicitors. A major gifts program cannot achieve success without the involvement of volunteers as leaders and solicitors. One challenge faced by small organizations with big missions is that their boards are often uncomfortable with major gifts fundraising (see Chapter 3). Recruited more for their program expertise than for their community connections, these board members often feel betrayed when suddenly they are expected to go out and ask for gifts face to face. Although, ideally, all board members would feel so intensely about the organization that they would find the ask a pleasure rather than a burden, such is rarely the case. Therefore, to have a major gift program that involves volunteers requires, in most organizations, having a separate major gifts team that solicits larger transforming gifts from individuals, family foundations, and corporations. Foundation fund-raising is largely the purview of the staff: When volunteers can provide needed linkage to foundation board members, call on them. (It is always good to know a foundation's policy on volunteer contact with board members—it can be the kiss of death in some foundations.) The major gifts committee is sometimes a subset of the development steering committee (Grace, 1997), but it can also stand alone. The subset model is used not only for managing annual major gifts, but also during a capital campaign, when it is the offspring of the campaign cabinet or the steering committee or council. In general, the duties of a major gifts committee or subcommittee are

- Identification of potential prospects through review of lists, silent prospecting (Grace, 1997), generation of names, and other activities
- Qualification of these prospects according to their connection with the organization and individuals within the organization, their capacity for giving, and their concern for the issue(s) the nonprofit addresses in its mission
- Development of a solicitation strategy, including cultivation activities, suggested gift amount, appropriate solicitor match and approach (the right person asking the right person for the right amount and the right purpose at the right time), and timing of the ask
- Create, or cause to be created, marketing materials that position the organization in the context of the issue being addressed
- Supervision of and participation in the cultivation process itself—both formal cultivation (lunches, tours, meetings, presentations) and informal cultivation (newsletters, notes with newspaper articles, copies of press releases, etc.)

- Evaluation at some point in the cultivation process to verify whether the strategy pursued is the correct one or whether a mid-course correction is required
- Solicitation of major gifts (see Chapter 9), pairing up with program and executive staff of the organization
- Implementation of the appropriate stewardship activities (see Chapter 11) that will convey to the donor that their gift was transformational, not transactional, and that you are as interested in a relationship with them as you were interested in their gift
- Evaluation of the whole process, and development of new strategies to keep the donors involved and/or to provide opportunities for them to increase or renew their investment.

4. Evaluate the program regularly.   A major shortcoming of many non-profits is the failure to take time to evaluate their development activities. Because organizations feel they must rush from donor to donor or from program to program, reflection on effectiveness seems like a luxury. Nothing, of course, could be further from the truth. In major-gifts fund-raising, there are many reasons to evaluate continually. These are related to

- The donor's relationship to the organization
- The quality of stewardship
- The effectiveness of the ask
- The appropriateness of the amount of the ask
- The continuing expectations of the donor regarding institutional performance
- The ways in which others like this donor can be brought in
- The effectiveness of organizational messages and mission definition
- Helpful feedback received during the process
- The way to convey to the community the impact of a transformational gift

Each of these evaluation areas can provide solid information for continuing to shape and build a powerful major gifts program. Don't ignore this step—it is essential for the organization's future major gifts planning. Chapter 12 explores evaluation more fully.

5. Link major transformational giving to the annual giving program, even during a capital campaign, and encourage ongoing synchronicity of annual and transformational major giving.   Because very large major gifts can and do transform organizations, the positioning of annual giving opportunities can take on new dimensions. First, the aggregate of repeated large annual gifts can provide new security to key programs, permitting them to increase their outreach and impact. With a steady new stream of annual funding, a clinic can increase its service area, a youth orchestra can expand its repertoire and membership, a homeless program can open another transition training center, and the case can be made ever more strongly that the need reflected in the mission is being met with increased impact.

Second, transformational gifts to a new or expanded facility or endowment further secures the program. Grace Cathedral in San Francisco, on completion of the cathedral close building project in 1995, found itself more advantageously positioned to attract program funding for parts of its vision that had remained only a dream—particularly the development of grace.com, their uplink satellite communications program. Other program funding followed, and now, as they find themselves in the midst of another capital campaign for restoration of the cathedral's stained glass windows, they are uniquely positioned for success because of their increased visibility through grace.com. The synergy of this kind of funding, particularly when guided by visionary goal setting and institutional planning, can lead to stronger organizations more capable of maintaining community programming. The synchronicity implicit in the ebb and flow of major gifts through annual and capital programs can only lead to greater institutional stability and community strength.

6. Promote the organization's results, not its needs. Transforming investments are made in organizations that donors believe have the resources and management to fulfill the intent of the gift. The only needs on which an organization should focus are the needs it is meeting. Nonprofits should be able to describe and quantify those needs, and state the strategies they are using to meet them. Investors buy into success. They want their gifts to transform, and they will select those organizations they feel are capable of producing change within the community. Nonprofits raise money not because they *have* needs, but because they *meet* needs (Grace, 1997). Furthermore, they should be proud of their successes, and should measure them by their impact on the community. Statistics that quantify service, when coupled with stories about some of those individuals who benefited from the service, convey powerful mission messages for investors.

A key tenet of successful major-gifts fund-raising is this: The organizations that raise and receive the most in major gifts are those that raise and receive the most in major gifts. We need only look at major universities and hospitals, at premier arts and cultural organizations, to know this is true. For smaller organizations with big, important missions the challenges are greater, but the principle is the same: Those that are accomplished at meeting needs and effecting change attract more gifts than those that constantly present a precarious financial situation and the need for money. Investors put their money into solid organizations that produce results. And, fortunately, thoughtful investors who believe in programming that may need a stronger organization to support it will often put money into capacity-building for that organization. They are protecting their investments, and ensuring a continuity of service delivery to the people and communities about which they care.

7. Approach each gift from the standpoint that it is transformational, not transactional. Developed more fully in chapter 1, this concept is another important one to put into practice. Transformational approaches are built on the premise that each investor begins a new and important relationship with the organization when the gift is made, and will be watchful, involved, and concerned as the impact of the gift is realized. Transactional approaches may fail to honor this need for a continued relationship, focusing instead on the gift transaction as the endpoint of the process of securing a gift rather than as the starting point in the process of involving the donor as investor. Stable major gifts programs—whether annual or in cyclical capital campaigns—are based on the overt or implicit acknowledgement of the transforming nature of the gift.

As a program, major gifts crosses both annual and capital giving, and is part of planned giving as well. In that respect, it is a result as well as a program.

MAJOR GIFTS AS A RESULT

A well-designed annual giving program is still a critical factor for some transformational giving. Even with increasing numbers of donors who begin with large gifts, then become involved with smaller annual gifts, perhaps repeating their large investments at intervals, it is still important to have the mechanism of a solid annual giving program in your organization.

An annual giving program provides the nonprofit with regular opportunities to test its mission in the community and to attract new donors who may have transformational gift or major gift potential. Annual giving is still the best, most regular source of unrestricted money for current program support. Further, a well-managed annual giving program builds donor confidence in the organization, and lays the groundwork for the donor's consideration of larger transforming gifts.

Major gifts—and those that transform—can then be viewed as a *result* as well as a *program*. The principles that guide annual programs are basically the same as those reviewed in this chapter for major gifts programs. However, when considering transformational gifts to be a result, we need to look beyond the mode of giving to the larger context a transformational donor considers.

The following five factors help encourage those with capacity, who might begin giving at a lower level, to make transforming gifts:

1. *Appropriate and regular stewardship, beginning with the first gift.* As developed in chapter 11, *stewardship* is more than a set of practices: It is a philosophy based on mutual respect for both the source and impact of the gift. If annual donors receive, from the outset, information and feedback about the impact of their gifts, they will be more willing later to consider larger investments.

2. *Continued focus on the issues addressed by annual giving.* Although it is easier to convey the impact of a transformational gift (e.g., a new building, wing, program, or endowment), it is also important to convey the transformational impact of the aggregate of annual giving and how the donor's investment, when combined with the investments of others, has made a difference. The kind of marketing and stewardship that works with transformational donors is precisely the kind of marketing and stewardship that are critical with annual donors who may grow into major donors. Focus on issues: how you are reducing hunger, alleviating the dangers and difficulties of homelessness, and so forth, and how annual gifts "from donors like you" make this possible.

3. *Good systems in place.* Donor tracking, with accuracy and timeliness, is a key factor in ensuring that major gifts will grow out of your other giving programs. Letters should reflect appreciation for previous gifts while asking for additional annual investment, and mailings should be personalized to the greatest degree. Thank-you letters generated within 24 to 48 hours of a gift make a huge impact on the donor. If that is not possible due to short staffing or a long weekend, pick up the phone and thank the donor, or send an e-mail or fax with a note that a proper thank-you is on the way.

4. *Personal involvement.* Begin personal involvement as soon as a person enters your donor arena. *Thankathons,* involving volunteers in phone calls that thank donors for their gifts, are a strong supplement to the required receipts and thank-you notes. The human voice is a powerful connector, and can convey warmth and appreciation like no other medium.

5. *True value-added impact from their gifts.* Donors sometimes become skeptical about whether their gifts are really needed by the organization. This impression may grow out of careless stewardship. As long as your organization is meeting community needs and can demonstrate that there are more needs that must be met, that you are focusing on the larger issue, and that you are committed to solving community problems or enhancing community resources, then the value-added aspect of giving will be satisfied. Simply to raise more money without visible indication that the money has been invested in programs that are stimulating change is not enough. People enjoy investing in successful organizations. Show how successful you are at meeting community needs, how the need continues or is growing, and why you are the best organization in which to invest. In the best of all possible worlds, most of our organizations would not exist. We would have solved the problems that plague us. Until all those needs are met, we need to promote our successes and invite investment.

CONNECTING PLANNED GIVING TO TRANSFORMATIONAL AND ANNUAL GIVING

Keep the connection with your planned givers intentional. They can become generous annual donors because they are already invested. They will want to protect their investment. Even if planned gift donors do not make annual gifts or direct transformational gifts, remember to provide the highest form of stewardship to them. They are investing in your organization for a time when they will not be there to see the impact of their gifts. A planned gift, for that reason, is the ultimate investment of trust; remember this in your stewardship and other development-related activities. Many people are uncomfortable with the concept of planned gifts as they struggle with their own mortality. It is up to nonprofits to assure them, once they make their gifts known, just how powerful their gifts are in the future planning for the organization. Part of the planned giving program needs to focus on encouraging people to communicate their estate plans. Handle these donors with sensitivity and discretion. By knowing about the gift, you are able to place them on the development continuum, providing them with stewardship and information that will give them confidence and satisfaction about their decision to make this long-term investment in your organization.

CONCLUSION

To ensure that mission-based, major transformational giving becomes both the result of an overall development program and a program in itself, stay focused on the issues, the impact, and the investment in all giving programs while implementing systems that will support accuracy, timeliness, and response. In so doing, you will enhance the overall mission of your organization. The effective community partnership among your organization, the community, and your donor-investors will not only be a *result* of concerted efforts, but will become part of an ongoing *program* of continual conversations with those who, through their nonprofit investment, can transform their communities.

Recruiting Donor-Investors for a Major Gifts Culture in the Nonprofit Organization

THE STATUS QUO

The American economy is cyclical, and when it slows down many non-profits realize that their budget projections will not be met. Because they have not planned for any fund-raising contingencies, they have nowhere to go: They have not recruited donor-investors and have no fund-raising strategy in place. Boards of directors of thousands of nonprofits in the United States have let themselves be lulled into accepting fund-raising programs that do not require asking prospects directly for donations.

The major gifts fund-raising program is on the tip of the classic fund-raising pyramid. All other fund-raising programs feed into it, and together they are known as the *annual development program*. This is the first step in creating a major gifts culture. The governing body of the organization must implement this comprehensive development strategy, including a major gifts program. Board members are the implementers of any strategic plan; they are the tactical force that makes the major gifts culture successful.

Most nonprofit boards are complacent—they like the status quo. Perhaps not all of the nearly one million-plus boards in the United States feel this way, but enough do that we can make the observation without fear of contradiction. The situation has existed for many years and will continue until the board members and executive directors (EDs) of these agencies get over the fear of being rejected by high-profile board candidates and begin to recruit aggressively volunteers who can become future board members and donor-investors. This is the single reason that thousands of non-profits lack a major gifts program, which means their programs cannot make an impact on communities. For years they have relied on other fund-raising programs to meet their budget needs. These other fund-raising programs—direct mail; telephone solicitations; bingo and gambling nights; and grants from foundations and from local, state, and federal governments—all have a common element: They are remote. No one, neither board member nor professional staff person, is asked to make a face-to-face solicitation, and complacency sets in again. Proactive volunteers, people who will do direct face-to-face solicitations, are required for organizations to begin and sustain a major gifts and transformational giving program.

Where do donor-investors come from? The board of directors, the ED, and senior professional staff form the nucleus of a planning process that brings together and energizes all of the nonprofit's recruitment resources. These include community programs, networking within and without the nonprofit's constituency, public relations, and marketing.

The recruiting process begins when board members and the nonprofit staff exchange the names of people they believe would enhance the agency's position in the community. Creative EDs who are active in their communities know candidates they would like to have as members of the board. Board members also know with whom they would like to associate. The following is an example of what they would like to achieve.

The Stern Grove Festival

The Stern Grove Festival is an excellent example of an organization with a board of directors composed of donor-investors who've created a major gifts culture that produces high impact philanthropy for their community. More than 60 years ago the Stern family donated a pristine grove to the people of San Francisco to be operated in conjunction with the San Francisco Recreation and Parks Department. The main proviso in the gift was that every summer a festival was to be produced, open free of charge to everyone who would like to attend. Now a 501[c] [3] nonprofit, the Association's board is still headed by a direct descendent of the Stern family. Many of the board members are from old San Francisco families. The board also includes professionals representing the community's opera, ballet, symphony, and avant-garde dance groups, and the corporate world of finance, law, and government. It is prestigious. It is envied. And, it is the paragon of a major gifts culture. This is the kind of board that will generate high impact philanthropy and transformational giving that benefits the community.

RECRUITING THE DONOR-INVESTOR

Frequently, nonprofit fund-raising runs in cycles. For many years board leadership typically took the agency from one new plateau to another, and they rode this wave of prosperity with an unending list of donor-investors, until one year they literally ran out of people and had no new leadership to whom they could pass the gavel. The existing board leadership continued out of loyalty, but they soon burned out.

At this point in a nonprofit's lifespan the ED commonly takes the reins until fresh new volunteer leadership can be recruited. Unless the ED is a person with leadership qualities and good standing in the community, all fund-raising slows down, and major gift fund-raising becomes almost nonexistent.

Not all nonprofits can emulate the Stern Grove Festival as an entertaining, free, community-wide institution with a prestigious board of directors. However, it is a goal to aim for, and a model to follow. If a nonprofit has been active in the community for more than a few years, it is assumed to be offering a value to the community. It has a following, and it has a board of directors with a minimum number of members that always needs an infusion of new people (ideally, donor-investors) and ideas to activate an ongoing, grass-roots fund-raising plan. Until recruitment has taken place, the establishment of a major gifts program is often not a realistic goal.

Based on these assumptions, a plan for the continued recruitment of board members and volunteers who will become donor-investors should be drawn up. Many potential donor-investors will want to support the agency, but not in a structured way; for example, they may not want membership on the board or formal committee assignments. Do not neglect these folks—they know many of the people the agency wants to recruit for the board of directors and they can arrange those introductions. Formation of a Committee on Trustees and the adoption of formal policies and procedures for recruitment, enlistment, evaluation, and retention of board members set the stage for action (Grace, 1997).

What are the characteristics of the people who should serve on the board? "[T]hey also guarantee a different kind of relationship—not a hit and run, but a mind-share involvement. If you're a stakeholder you give freely of your introductions and your time, your contacts. You're not hoarding."[1]

How does an agency find volunteers with a mind-share involvement—these donor-investors of the future? First, using the lists of poten-

[1]Sunny Bates, *New York Times,* March 29, 2000.

tial prospects that have been drawn up and categorizing the names on the list according to the two characteristics, a networking plan is created. Assignments to arrange for appointments are made, beginning with assigning each suggested board and professional staff to recruit to one of his or her peers. It is crucial that a potential prospect with the means to become a major giver and/or donor-investor and the potential to join the board talk to someone from the agency's board (if there is someone on the board who knows this person well enough to talk on a one-to-one basis).

If the prospect is not known to a member of the board and contact is made through a friend of a friend, make sure that the meeting has a social aspect—for example, luncheon or cocktails after work. The friend who is the go-between should be present; he or she should advise the friend (the prospect) that this is not a solicitation or recruitment meeting, but only an initial getting-to-know-you introduction. From this point on, the conversation, like most first-meeting conversations, should continue with chitchat aimed at finding a common ground, thus helping both participants begin to become comfortable with each other.

After the first meeting, the board member should know if the prospect is interested in great involvement, or if he or she should simply be placed on the prospect mailing list. A meeting that has gone well can be followed up by a letter acknowledging shared values, with agency brochures enclosed. The matter of who responds first will determine when the board member asks the crucial question: "Will you join our board?" If the prospect contacts the board member soon after the initial meeting, and in a positive manner, then at the next get-together the ED should attend and the crucial question can be asked during a very serious and frank discussion of the agency's mission and vision. If the board member must initiate the second meeting, the question should be put off until the prospect has met the ED and the rest of the board. This board member's intuition plays a large part in determining when and if the crucial question can be asked.

Another recruitment tool is the agency's *annual special event,* either a community dinner, a reception for the board or special guest at one of the board members' residences, or at a golf tournament or auction. An excellent example is the special-event testimonial dinner, at which a long-time volunteer of the agency receives a special award. If the event is produced with networking, marketing, and recruitment as three of its goals, then the board members are in an excellent position to talk to the guests and explain the work of the nonprofit with hundreds of supporters in attendance. Targeting specific guests who are on the board's number-one prospect list can be accomplished in a very casual and friendly manner, and the assigned board member can easily determine if the guest is interested.

With most successful organizations, recruiting volunteers and board members is a daily activity for the president of the board, the chairperson of the executive committee, and the ED. These three principal officers of the nonprofit have meetings with potential donor-investors during the normal work day. A board member, for example, might have a lunch meeting with his or her attorney, banker, or accountant, or with an executive of the company's largest vendor. The ED meets with many different people, ranging from those who want to know more about the work of the nonprofit to those who provide services for the agency. If these people are already involved, they can suggest others whom they know might be prospects. The ED should guide conversations so that the work of the nonprofit can be discussed comfortably with anyone he or she might meet, whether during the day or at evening gatherings. You should always be on the lookout for potential donor-investors and volunteers, especially when the agency is going through a difficult period of fund-raising. Remember that people give to nonprofits not to help the agency meet its administrative needs, but to further the programs that have an impact on the community.

A BLUEPRINT FOR RECRUITMENT

Chapter 4 details the internal and external case statement for transformational giving. The board members, the ED, and senior staff members of the agency should each keep with them, for easy access, a blueprint of the nonprofit's community programs. This blueprint should include

- An up-to-date mission and vision statement
- The agency's current program brochures
- The current fiscal year budget
- A list of members of the board of directors and the advisory board
- Special marketing materials that can fit into a handbag or briefcase

An additional item that can prove very useful is an agency business card printed individually for each member of the board and advisory group, with a brief description of the agency's goals on the reverse side of the card.

THE MAJOR-DONOR CULTURE AND HOW IT CAN AFFECT RECRUITMENT

Hardly a week passes without an announcement of a transformational gift from the Gates Foundation, Ted Turner, George Soros, or Steve Case, or from the one of the thousands of multimillionaires located in almost every region of the United States.

How does this infusion of mega-dollars affect your recruitment of potential donor-investors? If your nonprofit is the fortunate recipient of one of these mega-gifts, it benefits in at least two ways: (1) through the gift's impact on the agency's program (and on the community it serves), and (2) through the announcement of the gift in the local media—a marketing coup that will bring added recognition to the agency and will, in turn, make the recruitment process that much easier.

It is obvious that these donor-investors cannot sit on the board of every nonprofit to which they contribute. However, their transformational gifts can be and almost always are used as magnets to draw other donor-investors to the recipient agencies. Everyone likes to be associated with a winner, and nonprofit board members are no different. Association with an agency that receives a transformational gift can be just as prestigious as affiliation with the transformational giver.

CONCLUSION

Recruitment of those who will create a major transformational gift culture in your organization is essential in achieving high impact philanthropy. All nonprofits—from the old, well-established agencies to the newer ones—need to plan strategies that will increase the recruitment of donor-investors as advisors and to their boards of directors. To be successful and lead both to new major gifts and to strenghthening of the agency's programs in the community, recruitment must be an on-going job. Transformational gifts and any recognition the agency receives as a result of these gifts, can be used in its marketing effort, and ultimately will assist in the recruitment process.

4 Getting the Organization Behind the Transformational Giving Plan

Making the Case for Major Gifts

The case for major gift investments needs to be made to both *internal* and *external constituencies.* As organizations, we spend most of our time making the case to our external communities because that is where we find our prospects and where we fulfill our missions. However, to be effective in the cultivation and solicitation of major gifts among our external constituencies, we also need

- Strong internal support from administration and program staff.
- Board members committed to the development process.
- Staff resources (human and financial) clearly assigned to the development process.

Building the case for support internally is critical to the successful marketing of your organization externally. Both efforts are dependent on your ability to express your vision, values, and mission to people who will share them, help you share them with others, and invest in you. The basis for success comes from creating a culture in transformational giving (see

Chapter 3) through recruitment, and by the strength of the internal and external case for support.

THE INTERNAL VERSUS THE EXTERNAL CASE: PROCESS, CONTENT, AND USES

Case is defined as the sum total of all the reasons that someone should support your organization (The Fund Raising School). The case comprises both internal and external elements. With both internal case development and external case expression, the process and the content are part of the message.

Internal Case Development

Overview

Internally, the case is all the information you may have to provide for donor development, fund-raising, or marketing—your vision, mission, and goals; a description of your programs and services; background information on key personnel, board members, and their community affiliations; and a description of facilities and other resource information. This repository of information, though available, is seldom used in its entirety.

The internal case development process requires preparation of detailed materials by development and administrative staff and board (mission, vision, goals, objectives, board-member lists and descriptions, financial information) and the gathering of materials from program staff (program descriptions, profiles of key staff, service or attendance figures, special project descriptions). Your approach to these tasks, particularly with program staff, needs to be framed within the larger vision that these efforts support. The request for existing or new information should focus entirely on how this process supports the major gifts program and the benefits that program will produce. Staff and volunteers need to see that their participation has a direct impact on the potential ability of the organization to attract transformational gifts.

Nonprofits spend much time, money, and energy creating new ways to convey their messages—mission, vision, values, accomplishments—to their external constituencies. For some reason, we feel that our internal constituencies (board and staff) understand the message and are confident about sharing it with others. It is just as important (and maybe more important) to convey the same excitement and inspiration to our internal constituencies. Every board meeting, staff meeting, and retreat should feature ample product news that continually reminds those closest to you just why they got involved in the first place and why they want to keep working on your behalf. Following are some other ideas about keeping board and staff energized about the mission, thus ensuring the authenticity of their enthusiasm.

- At every board and staff meeting, include a short presentation by a client or someone else who has benefited from your programs or services. This is best done in the middle of the meeting to catch the latecomers and the early leavers.
- Feature a front-page article in every issue of your newsletter that focuses on the impact of your programs on the community or on clients.
- Send an occasional mailing from the chief executive officer or board chair to board members or key constituents, highlighting some singular impact the organization has made.
- Conduct briefings, on a regular basis, for staff and/or board about vision, goals, and accomplishments.
- Schedule strategic planning sessions, with regular updates and evaluations of the plan by both board and staff.
- Perform an internal review of the mission and vision every three to five years.
- Integrate the mission and vision into all of your internal communication materials.

These steps provide the platform for a successful major or transformational giving program. Through these efforts, organizations can increase the willingness of board and staff members to participate in the major gifts process, and thus can help ensure their confidence and expertise as advocates.

SUPPORT FOR THE CULTIVATION PROCESS

Another aspect of internal support for the case for major investment is the allocation of funds, through the budgeting process, to the cultivation of major prospects and to stewardship of those prospects once they become donors. While it is easy to see the cost-to-benefit ratio from (for example) a special event, direct mailing, or annual personal solicitation program, it is harder to measure the benefits of the cost of a cultivation event. Internal marketing of the major gifts process needs to involve the business or financial officer and the finance or budget committee of the board. The controller of one arts organization, unfamiliar with the major gifts process, wanted to assign funding for cultivation events to "Travel and Entertainment"—a line item that would have raised eyebrows had it been used. Cultivation and stewardship activities (the "before" and "after" of major gifts solicitations) must be budgeted if an organization is going to succeed with transformational gifts. If those responsible for the budget do not understand the long-term investment nature of cultivation and stewardship, they will be reluctant to approve a budget with those line items. The neglect of stewardship is the foremost cause of donor dropoff in nonprofit organizations. People who give their money and then are ignored will find another organization where they feel appreciated and involved. Likewise, those organizations unwilling to invest in the cultivation of prospective donors or who expect board members to fund all cultivation costs will have a lower fulfillment rate with their cultivation and solicitation efforts. Board members will be reluctant to continue such support, and will wonder why the organization, which stands to benefit directly from the major gift, is unwilling to make the investment in the cultivation process.

Generating and Maintaining Internal Case Materials

Nonprofits that keep their case materials current and accessible are able to respond to requests and opportunities in a timely way, thereby ensuring that potential funders or publicists have accurate information on which they can act.

Timeliness has never been more important than it is today. Those interested in and capable of making transformational gifts are frequently quite impatient for requested information. There is a new sense of urgency among those capable of making significant investments in our organizations. They are discovering the impact they can have through their nonprofit investments, and they expect our organizations to respond in a very timely way. Many are in a hurry to make the gift and start seeing results. Nonprofit organizations are in danger of losing gifts and confidence when they take too long to respond. Furthermore, because many emerging funders are motivated by issues and are less loyal to or familiar with institutions, they will become impatient with a process that is too lengthy. In their impatience, they will seek another, more responsive nonprofit that addresses the same issue. Some end up feeling they cannot access those organizations that are acting on the issues about which they are concerned, and ultimately quit trying.

Nonprofits must have their internal case materials accessible, in order, accurate, and complete at all times. This does not mean writing a lengthy document. The internal case is less a document than it is an ordered collection of information—a smorgasbord from which the desired material can be drawn and used in proposals and conversations with potential funders, for press releases, and in direct mailings.

The maintenance of the internal case is a responsibility shared among program staff, administration, and development, and must include narrative, financial, and graphic support materials. Changes in staffing or programs should be documented immediately and added to the internal case materials, and budget materials should be revised at least monthly. The case can be maintained on the computer, in a file, in a binder, or in any combination of approaches, as long as it is accessible. Some organizations prefer to have hard copies of all materials in a tabbed binder so they can easily make copies even when a computer and printer are not available. One agency kept three full sets of internal case information in binders that could be checked out by staff working on proposals.

When the internal case process, support, and content are given adequate attention and support, it is easier to take the case into the community.

External Case Expressions

External case expressions drawn from your internal case documentation must emphasize the community's need for your programs and services. The various expressions that are developed from the internal case include public relations materials, direct mail appeals, membership information, and major gift proposals. The translation is framed by the needs you *meet*, not the needs you *have*; by the purpose of the case expression; and by the intended audience.

In all case expressions, for whatever purpose, you should convey in some way the reason your organization exists. The "why" is the heart of the mission—it is the core expression of your values. A good way to test your ability to express this is by finishing the sentence "We exist because . . ." by describing the human or societal need that inspired the founding of your organization. By completing that sentence, you will not fall into an internally focused description of what you do; instead, you will end up describing the human or societal need that you are meeting. Follow that description with a statement of what you are doing to meet that need.

The following example of an external case expression was developed nearly a decade ago by Full Circle, a comprehensive agency in Marin and Sonoma Counties, California, programs designed to "work with families and children to prevent failure and abuse, or to provide help when serious problems already exist." Their prevention program serves school-age boys and girls; its residential program serves boys 10 to 16 years of age. Their mission-based program description captures a great deal about the organization, in strong persuasive language:

> At Full Circle, we have a clear purpose—to help children and their families overcome serious and complex problems.
>
> But keeping our goals simple, doesn't mean that meeting them is easy. Actually, the task of reorienting the lives of children and families is highly complex and intensive. It is satisfying to know that we are making a difference in a few hundred lives every year.
>
> We are proud of the fact that over the past 17 years our "success stories" have become productive members of society, raising families, running companies, or coaching Little League. We know that a single failure will cost the community hundreds of thousands of dollars—and that child's future.
>
> In a society with enormous problems, we have chosen to work one-on-one with people in need: when we help a youngster resolve his anger, we have made the world a less violent place to live. When we have helped a mom or dad parent more effectively, we have improved the whole family and tomorrow's families. When a learning disabled child starts to read, we may be unlocking the potential of a future Edison, Galileo, Einstein, or a fine next door neighbor.
>
> Full Circle Programs help solve some of the biggest problems faced by our society—child-by-child, family-by-family.[1]

Recent Changes in Case Expressions

Case expressions are increasingly less formal. First, even the most prestigious organizations are using printed text materials that are desktop published, limited in quantity, and highly tailored to the constituency for which they are intended. Second, organizations have increased their use of electronic media (videos, CD-ROMs, web sites/e-mail). The production costs of new media vehicles have been reduced dramatically, and the newer philanthropists are geared to respond. The use of printed materials is still important, but it must be balanced with other approaches.

Major changes have occurred in the development and use of all case materials, but particularly those used in major gift cultivation and solicitation. In working with these potential and continuing investors, use of printed materials is not nearly as important as personal interaction. Fur-

[1] Undated brochure, Full Circle, San Rafael, CA.

thermore as conversations are increasingly conducted via e-mail, we need to learn to get to the point. Even the briefest communication must be consistent in expressing the mission and purpose.

Paramount to our appeal to transformational donors is our ability to communicate our case to them in the manner that is most appropriate for them. Nonprofits know that the donor, not the organization, is the center of our universe, but we still tend to present our materials in the format and style with which we are most comfortable (or feel that we can afford). Now we must adapt to the styles of our donors. This requires us to maintain and practice a range of case communication strategies that we can quickly access for our potential donors. These include, but are not limited to

- An up-to-date, attractive, informative, and inspiring web site, with an interactive e-mail link so people can write or donate if they feel moved to do so
- Widely published web site information and e-mail address
- A newsletter, both mailed and available on the web site
- A listing with other web sites and information banks that deal with the same or related issues, so our organizations can be accessed by those who are interested in, for example, hunger, homelessness, child abuse, baroque music, etc.
- Draft proposals, including boilerplate information, stored in our computers so that tailored proposals can be generated in a timely manner
- Descriptive brochures to distribute to access points where people come with an interest in the issues we address
- Videos, audiotapes, and other media outtakes from programs that have featured your organization
- Other information that will be of interest to those who want to support your organization or learn more about it

MAKING THE CASE FOR TRANSFORMATIONAL GIFTS

To make the case for major or transformational gifts, organizations must be adept at expressing the external case points. Because we know that values are the basis of philanthropy, the external case for support must reflect the community values the organization advances through its work. Only then will it attract those donors who see in the organization long-term opportunities to act on their values.

Nonprofit organizations embrace core values that should form the guidance system for outreach, decisions, and donor satisfaction. Yet, because we know it is important to perform as a business and to survive the scrutiny of investors who are looking for a place to make a sound investment, we have too often given up our rightful place as the outspoken advocates of community vision and values. Although our organizations may act on those values daily, and extend that vision, what we say to our donors and convey to our communities is too often pitifully short on words that inspire.

Transformational donors are particularly motivated by values, and our dialogue with them as they are considering how, when, and how much to invest needs to be focused keenly on the values we represent.

FIVE PRINCIPLES FOR MAKING A VALUES-ORIENTED EXTERNAL CASE

Five basic principles frame the external case. They serve as the litmus test for any external case for support.

1. The external case should express the need you meet, not just the need you have.
2. If the mission is big enough, it does not matter that the organization may be small or brand-new.
3. Funders will measure their connections with you by the consistency and credibility of your values and how you act (or plan to act) on them.
4. The community's perception of your response to (or plans to respond to) the need you have identified will be critical in the decision to invest.
5. Your vision must have power and merit, and be relevant to the values of the potential investor and the community you serve.

MAKING THE CASE FOR TRANSFORMATIONAL GIVING: A CASE STUDY

Sage Hill School, a high school that opened in September 2000, in Orange County, CA constructed its case for support around these principles. From its inception, every decision and every gift has been guided by its vision and values: From the birth of the idea to the opening of the school, the consistency and integrity never faltered.

For the founding transformational donors, the message was clear. This was going to be a school that would encourage students to grow intellectually and physically in a diverse environment with opportunities to participate in service learning while pursuing a rigorous academic program. Conveyed initially through the thoughtful yet eager advocates who were its founders, the mission and vision of Sage Hill School eventually found its way into written materials and speeches delivered across the county.

These materials took the shape of newsletters, case statements, invitations, "view book" information for prospective students, a video, and other outreach. The speeches were given at informational meetings, independent school conferences, and before groups of potential investors. Derived from words and ideas generated by the founding board members, these messages were honed by the head of the school, by donors who gave feedback, and by the founders as they listened and watched hundreds of community members who came to organizational and informational meetings.

A new school builds itself on the foundation of what the community wants. The community wanted Sage Hill School—so much so that nearly $40 million was raised for the first phase construction and financial aid: fund-raising continues for the second phase of the physical plant, and for endowment.

Enthusiasm for the project is rooted to a large degree in community pride. Orange County has reached great maturity in the array of opportunities it offers in the arts, higher education, and social and human services. Although this was evident in many of its institutions, it was not present in secondary education. There was no independent, nondenominational high school. Those who sought that alternative for their children had to look to independent boarding schools in California or elsewhere. The time was right, but many families seeking an independent, nonreligious secondary high school for their children also had visions of a true alternative to the normal neighborhood clustering. They wanted a school more reflective of a county that is richly diverse in its ethnic and racial populations. They sought a location and a philosophy that would encourage and support an educational environment where students from all over Orange County could learn together.

These were the underpinnings of the founding values, and the founders were tenacious. Challenged persistently by those who did not feel such a vision was possible, the early believers kept advancing their dream. The result: Investors, including several transformational donors, were drawn by those values and willing to make investments.

Key Case Points that Matched Donor Interests and Values

The expressed values of the school's key donors ranged widely, but offered an array of case points which can be instructive to other organizations who wish to position themselves as appropriate investment vehicles for transformational givers.

- The fact that the school had long been needed, and that it fulfilled the educational dreams held for many years by those in the community
- A desire for the next generations of young people to have an educational experience that they themselves had not been able to have or had experienced in a similar school in another community
- A need to make a visible commitment to economic, social, racial, and ethnic diversity in what has been termed a private school with a public purpose
- A desire to be viewed as a community leader and investor in a school that would be leading-edge in curriculum, service learning, and leadership development
- A desire to give back to the community in which they lived and in which they had done well
- The wish that their children and grandchildren might have an excellent high school experience
- A desire to support other community leaders who were very invested in the development of the school
- A desire to fulfill a personal dream of being a major investor in the county's next great institution
- A wish to inspire others to invest
- A need to strengthen the community

These were the case points that appealed to the donors and matched their values. Ultimately, and most importantly, these points led to the donors' decisions that Sage Hill School was a good investment opportunity.

IDENTIFYING WHAT THE DONOR IS LOOKING FOR

It is not enough for institutions to want transformational gifts; they must also be perceived as appropriate organizations in which to invest. Increasingly, transformational and other major donors refer to their gifts as investments. They do not differentiate the giving process from that of their other investing. All that is different in their minds are the objectives and the results. However, just as they do with all their investments, transformational givers look carefully at the nonprofit organizations in which they are investing. They seek

1. Organizations and leaders with a clear vision and the capacity to enroll others in that vision
2. Organizations with a solid track record or promise of performance
3. A high potential for return on the investment, which for nonprofits is (a) continuation and growth of the values they honor, and (b) assurance of money invested and well spent with a high impact
4. Executive and staff personnel with integrity, expertise, and proven ability to deliver, which for nonprofits includes both the values and management sides of the organization
5. Opportunities to leverage their investments by attracting others with resources (of both time and money) into the organization
6. Timely and open response to inquiries about programs, finances, management, and investment growth opportunities
7. Regular information regarding the management and impact of their investments
8. Invitations to participate in decision making, particularly as it relates to their investments, which often includes a request to serve on the board or finance committee

POSITIONING YOUR ORGANIZATION FOR TRANSFORMATIONAL GIFTS

The competition for large transformational gifts is keen. Universities seem to be the most frequent choice for large donations, largely because their array of issues is much more wide-ranging than those of less complex organizations. Universities and colleges also have stronger infrastructures, leading investors to feel that there is greater safety in their investments. They are ideally positioned to attract transformational gifts because of their size, breadth, longevity (in most cases), and visibility. In many cases, there is also the attachment felt by an alumnus or teacher to an institution. Although the eventual investment may be issues based (for example, the gift of $100 million to the University of Mississippi from Jim and Sally Barksdale for literacy programs), the initial exploration is frequently based on a long-held personal attachment based on sentiment and experience.

Colleges, universities, established independent schools, and highly visible or venerable arts and cultural organizations have taken the lead in attracting transformational gifts. They have the staffs and the support to conduct consistent cultivation, the volunteers with whom to partner in the solicitation process, and the commitment to stewardship that leads to donor retention and increased gifts.

This does not mean that a smaller organization cannot attract transformational gifts; it simply means that it needs to present its issues both as its preeminent message and as an advantage of community investment. Donors seeking to solve or enhance community resource issues can see some great advantages in a smaller organization. They connect well to the motivations identified previously.

Smaller or less well-known organizations need to identify the qualities of those organizations that attract transformational gifts, and integrate applicable aspects into their own managements, leaderships, and structure. They then must convey these qualities to potential major donors. Some of these qualities are

- *Smaller* organizations actually offer greater opportunities for donor involvement than many universities and colleges.
- *Newer* organizations have the advantages of excitement, opportunity, heightened visibility and potential for impact, and lack of negative reputation (a problem for some established organizations), along with the greater opportunities for volunteer and donor involvement
- *Out-of-the-mainstream* organizations are attractive to some newer investors who have refined their giving interests to a particular niche. One young couple, Nicholas Lovejoy and Barbara Gordon, early participants in amazon.com, are turning their philanthropic energy toward sustainable urban gardens. By early 2000, they had capitalized their foundation (*New York Times,* Feb. 11, 2000) with $3 million and had given nearly $300,000 away to organizations in that niche market.
- *Emotionally, socially, and geographically* proximate organizations, no matter their size or visibility, have always attracted impact gifts from those devoted to them. This includes, in particular, organizations concerned with particular health, environmental, social, or diversity issues.

With smaller, newer, out-of-the-mainstream, or proximate organizations, the investor still needs to feel that his or her investment will be well managed with a high impact or return.

RESPONSIBILITIES OF DONOR-INVESTORS AND VOLUNTEERS

As those who are most often in the position to advance and validate the case and values of an organization to others, donor-investors, board members, and other volunteers have the responsibility to speak up when they feel the organization is drifting off course. *Mission drift* (Grace, 1997) is the primary cause of donor and volunteer disaffection; it is up to those outside the staff to provide an objective evaluation of the match between what the case says and what the practices are. Donor-investors, board members, and other volunteers need to practice responsible philanthropy. They need to

- Ask tough questions
- Press for evaluations
- Meet with key staff
- Get to know clients
- Speak up
- Speak out
- Give feedback, even when it may make the staff uncomfortable
- Ask for documentation and financial statements
- Participate in case review and validation
- Be supportive in times of crisis
- Be both advocates and asker-advocates

This level of involvement with the mission, vision, values, and case will mean a more stable organization in which further investments will flourish.

CONCLUSION

Making the case for transformational giving is both an internal and an external process. Although the obvious organizations are those of significant size, reputation, visibility, and infrastructure, other kinds of organizations should not feel excluded from the arena. To position themselves for major gifts, they need to make the case, as described in this chapter, and also to be sure they are

- Transparent in their disclosures of vision, mission, values, finances, impact, and strategic plan

- Relevant to the current needs of the community and capable of continually adjusting and changing to meet those needs
- Perceived as providing solutions and enhancements to urgent community needs or problems
- Accountable to their volunteers and donors through their programs and their reporting
- Well managed, well governed, and well publicized

These aspects lie within the reach of all organizations that want to attract and retain transformational gifts. They frame the case, and present it appropriately to the community.

PART II

THE NEW DONOR-INVESTOR

Major Donor Motivation

The Key to

Transformational Giving

A successful American business entrepreneur and his wife give a $100 million trust to his alma mater, University of Mississippi, the income from which will establish the Barksdale Reading Institute to raise literacy levels in that state. Another technology-industry billionaire Jim Clark, gives $150 million to Stanford University (where he formerly taught) to build a biotechnology center, crediting his experience there as a major factor in his later success. These gifts are front-page news. But there are other transformational gifts as well. A physician who practiced in a small town in Missouri leaves his estate of $12 million to the College of the Ozarks, whose campus was in the town where he practiced, because he admired the work ethic they instill in their students. A passionate hiker leaves $1 million in her estate to an environmental organization in California that is protecting an area where she spent many wonderful hours. The foundation of a royal family in the Middle East gives $250,000 to assist the research of a physician in San Francisco whose work on issues of aging has brought her international attention. A foundation in Colorado gives $250,000 to the Boys and Girls Club in a small town to build a youth center, believing that new resources must be made available to the children of that community. A foundation in the United Kingdom gives £2,000 to a program, previously funded only by its founder, to help children in Nepal who are jailed with their parents.

Tracking the motivations of these donors is not difficult. At the heart of each investment are values.

UNCOVERING MAJOR DONOR MOTIVATION

Values are the primary motivation for transformational giving. They guide donor development (the uncovering of shared values) (Grace, 1997) and inspire the stewardship and reporting that donors expect and to which they respond.

Years of observation, interviews for marketing and feasibility studies, and research conducted for this book reveal 10 prime values-based motivations of donor-investors. They invest in organizations because they want

1. To engage in issues that matter deeply to them and to their communities
2. To seed, encourage, or complete change
3. To leapfrog tiresome processes or bureaucracies (usually governmental) and get faster results
4. To give back to the community when their own assets grow
5. To ensure that others have what they have come to value and perhaps did not have earlier in life
6. To better their communities through development or enhancement of resources
7. To guarantee the continuation of ideas and institutions they value
8. To attain lifelong (and beyond) recognition through the establishment of endowments or the funding of capital projects
9. To affiliate with others having like values and interests
10. To be perceived as individuals and organizations who are making a difference, and to enjoy the resulting higher esteem

Exploring Each Donor Motivation

1. To engage in issues that matter deeply to them and to their communities. There is no disputing that philanthropy is increasingly issue-based. A singular sign of this trend is the rising number of foundations and individuals who will not accept requests from nonprofits; rather, they identify and approach those organizations that are dealing effectively with the issues that are important to them. This has major implications for the way nonprofits market themselves (see chapter 10). Our sector has not organized to market itself around issues. Donors complain that they want to get involved with, for example, organizations that work locally, regionally, nationally, or internationally with children of people who have been imprisoned. Finding such organizations is not easy, because we don't sort according to issue, and many organizations' names do not reveal their mission or purpose. If we are to tap into this strongest of motivations, we need to identify each of our organizations according to issue.

Donors of transformational gifts not only wish to support organizations that are addressing issues important to them, they often want to become deeply engaged through board membership or other involvement.

Nonprofits that have not made the requisite thinking shift required in the new partnership among organizations, donor-investors, and communities sometimes resist the involvement of transformational donors, fearing they will have undue influence. Our sector needs to come to terms with the donor's need to be involved in organizations, and we need to understand their motivation for involvement. This is not a matter of selling a board seat: It is the nonprofit equivalent of working with a corporate investor who wants a seat at the table where decisions will be made that affect his or her investment. The need for donors to become engaged with those organizations in whose values and programs they have invested is also developed elsewhere in this book. It is important to understand the intensity of this motivation among donors.

2. To seed, encourage, or complete change. A quick scan of web sites that have been created to attract direct contributions to various organizations reveals the extent to which we are beginning to understand and how much of a donor's motivation is the need to be a part of change. One web site is called *giveforchange*. One national organization has considered a new slogan for attracting donors and interest: "Want to buy some change?" The urge to change those things in society that either don't work well (for example, public education in America, which has attracted increased private funding) or could work better (medical service delivery into developing nations is huge. The idea of transformational giving is closely tied to the idea of change or, as previously stated, to the idea of making a difference.

Soliciting transformational gifts is also about change—raising the visibility of an issue (literacy in Mississippi) onto the public horizon, with the anticipation that others will also want to make an investment. For these donors to stay motivated they must be able to observe the changes made by their gifts. Donor stewardship must pivot around the indicators of change produced by the gift, and all messages to the community should be focused on the ways in which the issues are being more effectively addressed. Track and report measurable results: people helped, lives changed. Learn to tell stories that give life to your statistics. People remember them, and they tell them to others.

3. To leapfrog tiresome processes or bureaucracies (usually governmental) and get faster results. This is a good-news bad-news motivation for giving to our sector. Long viewed as the third sector—an effective alternative to the government and corporate sectors—the nonprofit sector has been seen as an effective agent of change. The confidence in our sector is a key aspect of this golden age of philanthropy, and many of our organizations—universities in particular—are benefiting as never-before imagined from the issue-driven, values-focused giving that has characterized the late twentieth century and the beginning of the twenty-first.

This is all good news, but the bad news lurks closely behind. One major donor-investor in a community, well known for his support of the arts, expressed frustration at trying to give to other institutions because of all the "process" he was put through. He finally gave up. We need to make sure that our internal systems are designed to encourage, not discourage, potential donors. Think through the various ways people access your organization.

- How well informed is the person who answers the telephone?
- How knowledgeable are your volunteers about your successes, your programs, your impact?
- Are you willing to bypass or accelerate processes to match the urgency a donor might feel about making a gift?
- Do you have a commitment to follow-through that ensures timely and appropriate responses to requests for information?
- Do you have a cadre of trained and willing volunteers who are peers of potential donors, who can respond immediately with enthusiastic encouragement about the benefits of giving to and being involved with your organization?

Those with major assets are frequently impatient to see results from their investments. There is an increasing tendency of the wealthy, when they are thwarted by a bureaucratic response to their interest, or their calls are not respected or returned, to leapfrog (there is even a foundation with that name) over existing institutions and go directly into communities to set up programs. This is a major warning signal, and one the nonprofit sector should heed. Nonprofits need to adapt their systems and structures to accommodate and encourage the donor who wishes to make a swift, effective, and important investment in an organization dedicated to the things he or she cares about. In this way the nonprofit sector holds up its corner of the three-way partnership among donor-investors, nonprofit organizations, and the community.

4. *To give back to the community when their own assets grow.* This is one of the oldest and most frequently recognized motivations among major and transformational donors. People like the idea of giving back—particularly when they themselves have benefited from the same kind of educational, social, cultural, health, or other programs at an earlier point in their lives. This is a primary motivation among many who give annual or endowed scholarships to their schools or universities. The student who studied on scholarship and then became hugely successful in life will often set up scholarships so that others can have the same opportunity. This is the most easily self-identified motivation. People are very connected to that value within themselves. Giving back makes the donor feel fulfilled, and is a very personal motivation.

To keep these donors motivated, provide a connection between them and the people they are helping. One donor to a youth facility in a beleaguered and crime-ridden suburb calls nearly every day to find out how many young people are using the facility, and to hear their stories. Wise scholarship administrators learned long ago the value of connecting donors and recipients; one university we know of goes a step further and connects grateful *parents* of scholarship students with the donors.

5. To ensure that others have what they have come to value and perhaps did not have earlier in life.   A very successful couple who, earlier in their lives, were not as connected with their Jewish heritage, have come increasingly to value that heritage. They have acted on their values by establishing a Center for Jewish Studies at the university they both attended. Many who emigrated to America from Europe and Asia during the latter part of the twentieth century have returned to their countries of origin to establish schools, hospitals, or cultural resources in the towns and villages where they were raised. A dentist of Chinese descent in California has established schools in China, and now regularly takes other interested people (most of whom are not Chinese) on journeys to China to see the impact of his philanthropy and get them involved as investors. Nonprofits that benefit from gifts given for these reasons will, again, emphasize the impact of these gifts through both statistics (how many served, how many attended) and stories (a child whose life was changed, a student who discovered the deep roots of his own Jewish heritage and launched a scholarly pursuit that changed his career focus).

6. To better their communities through the development or enhancement of resources.   This is often the motivation when significant corporate investment is directed by the CEO or chair of the corporation. Those corporations who are deeply invested in their communities are reflecting a corporate priority to enhance the communities in which they operate (to give back) and to provide high visibility for themselves as good citizens. Individual investors with this motivation are often those who have made their fortunes because of their successes in that community. Gauging this motivation in corporations is easy; it may not be as evident in individual donors.

7. To guarantee the continuation of ideas and institutions they value. Major investments are often driven by a commitment to maintain the ideas and institutions the investors value. One striking example of this took place at Mills College in Oakland, California. A venerable and respected women's college, its status as a single-sex educational institution was threatened by the economic realities of decreased enrollment. Many women's colleges on America's east coast had gone co-ed and Mills College seemed certain to follow. The board, however, was determined to maintain Mills' status as a women's college. Mounting a quick and quiet campaign—approaching board members, alumnae, and non-alums—the board raised sufficient funds to maintain its women-only status for the short term. It also launched a larger campaign to ensure its long-term ability to retain its singular status. While many of the transforming gifts of $1 million or more were from alumnae, many were from men and women who had never attended Mills College but who felt that the presence of this educational alternative was important to the overall educational opportunities both in California and nationally.

In a similarly transforming investment (in this case, one of time, not only of money) the current president of South Africa, Thabo Mbeki, when he was foreign minister, agreed to become the chair of the annual fund for his alma mater, the University of Sussex at Brighton, England. By lending his involvement and his already well-known name to what was then a fledgling program, he all but insured its immediate visibility and long-term success. His messages were authentic, and gave credibility to a program that was new not only to the University, but, at that time, to English universities in general.

8. To attain lifelong (and beyond) recognition through the establishment of endowments or the funding of capital projects. For some reason, most people are reluctant to admit that their motivation for giving capital and endowment gifts of significant size is recognition during their lifetimes and beyond. It is always refreshing when people can speak honestly and comfortably about their need to be recognized. One donor, open about his motivation, added a spin to it that may reveal another important dimension of this motivation. When considering a capital gift to his alma mater, this African-American attorney evaluated the possibility of naming it for his grandfather, who had been an immense influence in his life, and/or for his father, who had attended the same university. In the end, he had the building named after himself because, as he told a national audience at a conference in Washington, D.C., "I wanted people to know how much I cared."

In San Francisco, Louise M. Davies Hall, which houses the San Francisco Symphony and hosts other touring music organizations, was named after a spunky and outspoken civic volunteer who made the leadership gift to the capital campaign and who, with the gift, wanted to establish her identity as a philanthropist. She and her husband, Ralph K. Davies, had named other buildings and projects in San Francisco, but none of them bore her name alone. For the remainder of her long life, she cherished her decision and its result. Now, several years after her death, an expansion is planned for the symphony hall that will take over an open parking and utility area that has been lovingly known as "Lake Louise."

Critics of recognition-motivated giving seem to be looking for some more altruistic motivation—a curious pursuit. The motivation to be recognized for caring deeply about a community is frequently seen as the motivation to be recognized, period. One result of this kind of giving is the leveraging of gifts from others. The influential name on a building, or on a list of donors, is read avidly by those receiving an invitation or annual report, or by those waiting for a concert or event to begin. Some people are very persuaded by who else is making major gifts. That is part of *their* motivation. For individuals and institutional funders who are motivated by knowing that others know what they have done, be sure that the recognition is consistent and accurate. Increasingly, ethical issues regarding continued recognition by naming donors have emerged. Museums that change buildings, schools that move campuses, or buildings that are significantly altered by renovation or remodeling find themselves seeking new, naming donors to fund their moves or construction. They struggle with how to recognize the donors who had made the previous or original building possible. At the time gifts are made, conditions for continued recognition need to be discussed and agreed to. Otherwise, the families of earlier donors will be hurt and angry over the discontinuation of the name recognition. A basic policy should be in place, one that is appropriately guided by the reality that people don't give to buildings, they give to issues and institutions for which the building or endowment is the visible symbol. The importance of the original investment, even if the size is dwarfed by the size of gifts now being given, should never be publicly diminished. The gift, when given, enabled the organization to become the organization it now is. Respect for that investment should continue throughout the life of the organization. How that respect is shown is a matter for board decision.

9. To affiliate with others having like values and interests. This is a strong motivation. People like to be with others who care about the things they themselves cherish. People who fund the arts like to be with others who are devoted to the arts; it is the same for people with a strong interest in the environment, global health or economic issues, children, education, religion, or other matters. Affiliation with others of like motivation and values is a major reason people might give transformational gifts. They feel united with these other individuals, particularly if they are also major or transformational donors. This is true both in America and in Europe, where private-sector participation in educational, social, environmental, cultural, and human service institutions is on the increase. There is power in numbers, and people feel they have more leverage when they can share their passion with others.

10. To be perceived as individuals and organizations that are making a difference, and to enjoy the resulting higher esteem. Many of us live in communities whose resources, infrastructures, and institutions support our ability to establish and maintain a certain quality of life. Many of those investors who contribute to the educational, cultural, health, and social service institutions that create strong communities do so because they want the higher esteem that will follow. They like to be recognized for what they invest in their communities. National Philanthropy Day, celebrated in November across America, recognizes those investors, volunteers, nonprofit leaders, and others who make a difference. In France, those who give generously of their money and time are recognized with the Legion d'Honneur—an indication of the way in which philanthropy is increasingly regarded in that country. Although some may criticize this motive as self serving, it is important not to condemn as inappropriate or less noble any motivation that comes from an honest effort to build community resources. As long as the motivation is honest, and no harm or deception is involved, then it is the job of the nonprofit to ensure that the appreciation provided to the donor-investor is centered around the motivations that led to his or her gift. If, over time, these motivations change, then so should the stewardship and reporting of the gift's impact.

MAINTAINING DONOR MOTIVATION

To maintain donor motivation, and encourage increased participation, sharpen your communication of these five indicators:

1. *Program impact.* What difference has the gift made on the program? What difference is the program making in the community? What difference is the organization making in the community because of this program?

2. *Financial performance.* How effectively has the investment been used or managed? If it is a capital or endowment gift, how well is it being invested? Are your financial statements accurate and timely?

3. *Return on donor investment relative to the values the donor cares most about.* Look back on the list of motivations. Assign one of these motivations to your major donors, the ones you are cultivating for transformational gifts. Think of the other people in the community who could make a transformational gift to you, and assess their motivations. Then, think of how you could make their return on investment such that they would keep investing. If the motive is to change human or social conditions in your community or, through you, globally, could you produce results that would lead to greater investment? If the motive is to give back, do you have the stewardship mechanism in place to provide feedback that will assure the donor-investor of the impact of the gift? If affiliation and recognition are prime motivators, are your organization's systems geared to provide opportunities for affiliation and programs for recognition? Are your board and staff philosophically committed to true stewardship, or is your program limited to the perfunctory recognition more suited to transactional giving?

4. *Responsiveness to changes in the marketplace and within the organization.* The world outside a nonprofit's windows is constantly changing. To persuade donors effectively to maintain a transformational investment in an organization, nonprofits need to demonstrate they are observant students of this changing world and willing to make, initiate, and respond to change. Hanging on to old systems and structures that impede your ability to meet the fast-changing needs of the community is a sure way to dampen the energy of someone wanting to invest in you. Likewise, if changes occur in your organization due to death, departure, or dismissal, how effectively do you handle them? Does your response to internal and external change enhance the strength of the mission by demonstrating that it is your decision base and guide, or do you flounder and flutter and lose precious time and resources by not having the ability to act decisively and appropriately in the face of change? As nonprofits, we are community and investor partners and we are change agents. Yet, too many nonprofits are unable and unwilling to make changes that are required in order to serve their communities effectively and provide the highest possible return to their investors.

5. *Willingness to plan continually and to hone systems and structures.* Does your organization have a three-year strategic plan with a rolling base (so that every year, the just-completed year is evaluated and dropped and a

new year added)? Do you do a zero-based planning session every three or four years to take the organizational thinking down to zero and ask yourselves, "Given the needs in this community, what programs should we keep, start, or phase out?" Do you use your budget as a critical evaluation tool for all programs? Are you willing to make changes before you are told (by board or funders) to make them?

THE NONPROFIT MOTIVATION: TRANSFORMING DONORS, TRANSFORMING COMMUNITIES

The focus of this chapter has been on the motivations of donor-investors, and how organizations can and should encourage those motivations by positioning investment opportunities in such a way that donors feel fulfilled through the act of giving. These donor-investors, advocates for the communities in which they live or for which they want to provide services or programs, catalyze the nonprofit's ability to serve and strengthen communities. The partnership among nonprofits, communities, and donor-investors flourishes when each communicates and contributes in the most appropriate way: communities, by providing comprehensive needs analyses that are continually updated; nonprofit organizations, by providing services and programs that meet these needs; and donor-investors, by providing transformational and other gifts that ensure the ability of the nonprofit to deliver on its mission.

Ultimately, the reason and motivation for the entire nonprofit sector—including its organizations, the communities whose needs they meet, and the donor-investors who make transformational gifts—is to strengthen society. Furthermore, because nonprofits serve as the vehicle or delivery system, that *must* be the most salient motivation for nonprofits. In all our work, that motivation must govern. In our commitment to strengthen society, we will serve both our donor-investors and our communities well.

CONCLUSION

Values drive the motivations of donor-investors to make all gifts, especially transformational gifts. Complex and varied, ten prime values-based motivations have been identified through observation and research. To understand fully how to approach donors, nonprofits must understand their motivations; to keep these motivations vibrant and renew the investment, nonprofits must provide information and feedback that assure the donor that the ideas and issues that motivated them in the first place are being addressed, and that perceptible changes are occurring. Philanthropy is a partnership among communities, nonprofit organizations, and donor-investors, and the overall motivation of these partners is to strengthen society. Nonprofit organizations are the mechanism that assures the connection between the donor-investor and the community, and as such they must be accountable, dedicated to facilitating change, and able to adapt their systems and structures continually to the changing needs of donor-investors and communities.

6 ▼ The Impact of Major Gifts on Organizations and Communities

The subtitle of this book says it will tell you how donors, boards, and non-profits can transform communities. This is only one side of the equation. The other side is how the community itself sets the stage for creating and sustaining nonprofit organizations. The following questions will help clarify the community's role in the philanthropic world:

- How can your community benefit from the high impact philanthropy model?
- What would happen to the community if the nonprofit disappeared?
- Why are similar agencies providing the same program in one community?
- What is the relationship between the community and the independent nonprofit agency?

HOW CAN YOUR COMMUNITY BENEFIT FROM THE HIGH IMPACT PHILANTHROPY MODEL?

High impact philanthropy affects every person who lives in the community. In the United States, high impact philanthropy from donor investors funds community activities: religious, educational, health-related, human services, arts, public- and social-benefit, environmental, and even international causes. This is a partnership among three equals, if not in actual dollars, then in stature. The community makes the nonprofit welcome by fostering a climate that helps the nonprofit excel in its endeavors. Some communities have taxed tourists and have used those funds to support the nonprofit community (in San Francisco, the hotel tax is used for this purpose). The nonprofit can and often does make the community shine by using this welcoming attitude to produce performing arts, ballet, opera, and symphony, which draw these same tourists to the community year after year. In fact, all of the various types of nonprofits can produce programs to enhance their communities' reputations regionally, state-wide, and nationally.

The third partner in making all of this possible is the donor-investor who contributes major funds to support the community's nonprofits. The donor-investor gives to nonprofits on many levels: individually, through business and corporate affiliations, through self-established and self-operated private foundations, and through the local community foundation. In fact, community foundations in the United States make very large donations—the top 25 foundations fund nonprofits from a minimum of $15 million to a maximum of $144 million each year.[1] Put together, the individual and private foundation (individual and family) giving, and the impact on the community is huge.

Under the high impact philanthropy model the donor-investor funds the nonprofit, the nonprofit helps the community, and, in turn, the successful community makes a warm home for the nonprofit and the donor-investor. We must also consider government grants to the community, however. Locally funded programs that begin in the community may end their journey at the national level. For example, a program that helps people get back to work after they have been laid off puts those people back on the tax rolls. People who rejoin the working world are placed back into our economic culture, which recycles the funding from the top level as proceeds from income tax payments. The round trip from local to national or vice versa can be described in very simple terms: The nonprofit receives start-up funding from the city or state, which receives it from the federal government, which receives it from individual and corporate taxes. The basic seed grant helps the nonprofit establish or continue a community program.

WHAT WOULD HAPPEN TO THE COMMUNITY IF THE NONPROFIT DISAPPEARED?

Nonprofits disappearing? Yes—they do sometimes simply fade away, close the doors, even go bankrupt. Sometimes, however, they join forces

[1] The Foundation Center, 2000

and jointly sponsor a program with another nonprofit, or even—like for-profits—merge.

In the extreme, if a vital community nonprofit closed its doors because of lack of funding from either the public or private sectors, then obviously the community would lose an important organization and a community asset. One of the goals of this book is to prevent that from happening.

An article in the *San Francisco Chronicle* was headlined, "Financial Crisis May Close Oakland [CA] Aid Group."[2] For the previous four years this nonprofit had been providing some 15,000 disabled and elderly people in the community with recycled health equipment. The executive director was quoted as saying, "We're basically out of money in July." Their main source of funds turned out to have been a county agency, which had been providing annual grants of $112,000; quid pro quo, the county was saved space in its landfill, because the equipment that would have been thrown away if not for the nonprofit would have taken up a lot of space. Recycling the exercise equipment helped reduce the 1.6 million tons of garbage the county had to dispose of each year. A spokesperson from the agency was quoted as saying: "We really want them to succeed. We can't promise to be their only source of funding forever and ever. We have invested in them, and we want that investment to succeed." The article also mentioned that the nonprofit had received some support from private foundations.

The executive director's plan of action was to call on private foundations ". . . and other groups." There was also mention of a network of 300 doctors, nurses, and other healthcare professionals who encouraged hospitals and families with used equipment to donate it to the group. What was not mentioned was the name of any member of the board of directors, or any coherent fund-raising development plan.

The article ended with information on how to contact the nonprofit—not for funds, but to make equipment donations, which were accepted only on Mondays and Wednesdays. A telephone call made to the number printed in the article reached a canned message that informed the caller how to donate equipment. There was no mention of how to talk to someone about making a donation.

The community's loss of this nonprofit will be felt by many deserving people. This agency discovered a need in the community and devised an ingenious way to fill it, thus helping the community in two important ways. We can imagine that it is a very small organization with few employees, depending on volunteers to help recycle and repair the much-needed equipment. The irony is that this nonprofit is located in the midst

---

[2] Benjamin Pimentel, *San Francisco Chronicle*, June 30, 2000, page A25

of many organizations that can help. Northern California has many community organizations that, for a very few dollars, will come to the aid of an agency doing this type of service for the community.

This is why we have stressed the paradigm of *transformational* giving by donor-investors. Note the role of the *donor-investor:* Although public grants are manna from city, state, or federal heaven, to continue to grow and thrive you must recruit lay leadership who are also donor investors. Without a base of support from a natural constituency, nonprofits soon find that grants have a nasty habit of drying up after one or two years. The grantors want to see broad-based local support. Why? Because grantors (i.e., public and private foundations) are not in the business of funding agencies that do not grow—and this doesn't mean budget growth as much as it does keeping programmatic sharpness and being on the cutting edge of the mission statement. This can happen only with a group of concerned board members who take leadership roles with the agency. The catalysts in this situation are the executive and development directors.

The agency's executive and development directors guide the board of directors through a stewardship process to a higher level of giving, using the grants from the government as a platform for the community values exchange that is desired. The professional staff explain to the board that they cannot rely only on the largesse of grants from the various government agencies or private and community foundations. This explanation often is supported by a *strategic plan,* a concrete set of goals and objectives to which the agency must adhere if it is to survive. One tactical part of the strategic plan is recruitment. Lay leadership must expand their natural constituency and recruit their peers to be a part of this program, to give not only financial support, but their advice and knowledge. They become partners in transformational giving.

WHY ARE SIMILAR AGENCIES PROVIDING THE SAME PROGRAM IN ONE COMMUNITY?

As the nineties came to a close the media took a look at the changes in the demographic makeup of the United States. What did they find? Diversity—refugees from every area of the world have been flying, sometimes swimming, to our shores. They bring with them skills and a desire to share in every opportunity this country offers. They may be unprepared, however, for the ills that a free country offers its citizens in addition to the joys. For example, those who newly call the United States home are often very family oriented, and may have brought their parents and even grandparents, thus contributing to the already overcrowded senior facilities. Because of the diversity of their populations, these facilities need workers who can speak Spanish, Russian, Vietnamese, and Croat, just to name a few.

The AIDS epidemic has also fostered a unique set of problems, so that one often finds several AIDS-related agencies in the same community. Each may seem to accomplish the work, albeit with overlapping services, but a closer look reveals that the clients they serve have different socioeconomic and medical problems that are not being met by any of the agencies.

These tales explain why some agencies that appear to be doing the same work are, in realty, very different. If your nonprofit falls into a category similar to that of another nonprofit, you must take great care to explain the difference between that agency and your own to your lay leaders and potential supporters. Part of this process is maintaining an ongoing marketing strategy, as we explain more fully in chapter 10.

WHAT IS THE RELATIONSHIP AMONG THE COMMUNITY AND THE INDEPENDENT NONPROFIT AGENCY?

You may wonder why a number of nonprofit agencies are doing what appears to be work that the municipality could do, and maybe should do. In effect, local and state governments are hiring the agencies to do work that, because of politics and other social encumbrances, would cost the government entities a lot more money. Another problem is the independent streak of many professionals who cannot work with the arcane rules they would encounter in working for a government agency; similarly, creative people may struggle with the political agenda that is part of our government.

The independent nonprofit maintains its freedom within the conditions of the government grants it accepts, but it does depend on these grants. As previously mentioned, however, these grants from government and private sources have been known to shrink or simply disappear. To achieve full freedom from government funding, the nonprofit must raise its own funds. The high impact transformational strategy discussed and suggested in this book will allow the nonprofit to become its own master.

THE GOLDMAN INSTITUTE ON AGING: A CASE STUDY

In 1975, only one institution in the United States trained post-resident physicians to work with an increasing population of people over the age of 65. The concept of adult daycare centers was just beginning to be discussed. Lawrence Z. Feigenbaum, M.D., an internist and cardiologist by training, had recently moved from private practice to the position of chief of the outpatient clinic at Mount Zion Health Center in San Francisco. It soon became apparent to him that many of the elderly patients at the clinic had only a few choices when it came to extended care. These were people who did not require extensive nursing, but only assistance with meals, a place to meet and socialize with other people, and an activity to keep them occupied so that they were not literally bored to death. Either they had to have the funds for private workers to visit their homes, or they could go to a private or public care facility—and there were only a few of those available, with long waiting lists.

Feigenbaum learned that grant money was available through the federal Department of Health, Education, and Welfare (now called Health and Human Services.) The hospital applied for and was awarded a grant for a demonstration project; that went so well that the project was recognized by the Kaiser Foundation, which encouraged Mount Zion to submit a proposal for training gerontologists. Mount Zion received a grant for the training of post-resident fellows for one or two years; it was the second such program in the United States. Between 1975 and 1983 the program was part of Mount Zion Health Center, and was managed by a planning council made up of physicians, business executives, nonprofit foundation managers, and politicians. By that time, Feigenbaum had talked to and piqued the imagination of two community activists, and over one million dollars had been pledged for the start of a new nonprofit organization: The Institute on Aging (IOA). Soon after the doors opened, Feigenbaum solicited an endowment gift for the establishment of an adult daycare center. This placed the IOA on the map in San Francisco, giving the organization a bricks-and-mortar home and an identity in the community. The marketing of a nonprofit organization that interacts with people, whether in the field of health or the performing arts or as a helping-hand agency, requires a physical structure (either a long-term lease or its own building) to create an identity so that it can expand its place in the community's awareness for future development.

The IOA's adult daycare center is a named facility, and the donor continues to give substantial gifts each year. In this case the donor did not want to participate on the agency's board or take a leadership role in the organization. However, naming the facility for the donor-investor helped increase that individual's personal impact on the community and the nonprofit. Board members, major givers (current and potential), and the agency's lay leadership witnessed the impact they could make, either individually or through their business and private foundations. Although the person who makes a large gift for a named facility may not want to (or is unable to) give of his or her time with committees and the like, his or her name on the front door works 24 hours a day to remind all who pass by that there are opportunities for everyone to become investors with the nonprofit.

The Goldman Institute on Aging (GIOA) has one lay leader who both has been the model for and defines the transformational profile we have been discussing so far. This person has been associated with the GIOA since its inception; he was the first president of the board and has served on practically every committee as an active participant or chairman. He has helped recruit board members and lay leadership, and has given the professional staff advice on business matters that they could receive only from a person who has many years of experience as an executive with a major corporation. He makes leadership gifts every year, and networks in the business community for the agency. Most important of all, he has the best attendance record at board and committee meetings of any lay leader supporting the organization. He can be counted on. He invested in the GIOA and is now a donor-investor.

The GIOA has a number of programs specifically designed for new board members, current givers with the potential to upgrade to the "major" category, and prospective major givers. Board orientation meetings are not a new concept. Many nonprofits use this technique to introduce a newly elected board member to the intricacies of the organization they have agreed to support with their time and money. The difference with the GIOA's orientation is the steps it uses to welcome and guide the new board member through the many programs the GIOA operates in the community.

The first step in the GIOA's orientation is the orientation binder, which contains the following descriptive documents:

1. Side one
   a. GIOA bylaws
   b. A statement of what is expected of board members
   c. Fiscal year budget (audited)
   d. Current annual report
   e. Biography of each board member

    f. List of board members including addresses, telephone and fax numbers, and e-mail (each for both home and work)

    g. A list of board committees

2. Side two

    a. Mission statement (also presented on the outside of the binder)

    b. A one-page description of each GIOA community program

    c. President's presentation

The next part of the orientation is the tour program. New board members, major gift prospects, and prominent citizens (politicians, etc.) are taken on a series of tours of each of the GIOA's community programs. No reading of position papers can take the place of an actual tour of an in-place, running program, where the board members can meet the professional staff and, most importantly, the people who are being served.

The GIOA's orientation program is an example of stewardship at its highest level. This type of orientation is easily accomplished with health, educational, and service types of nonprofits. Nonprofit arts organizations and the artists who participate in them (e.g., painters and sculptors who exhibit in museums) sometimes resist programs such as this because they fear that bringing strangers into the studio or performance hall will disrupt them. Yet, of all the types of nonprofits, art institutions best lend themselves to interaction with their nonartistic supporters. If carefully planned, these in-depth tours will benefit not only the nonprofit, but also the artists, who often feel isolated from the people who support them.

Unless you are part of an enormous organization, your thoughts at this point might sound something like this: "We are nowhere near large enough to give tours of our agency." "No one with that kind of money is affiliated with our organization, let alone sits on our board!" "Your ideal investor is too ideal. In our community people like that don't even exist." "Our board is composed of ordinary, middle-class citizens who volunteer their time and give what money they can afford. Some of them may be employed by large corporations, but these companies are headquartered in the large cities, far away from our small community."

If you're thinking along these lines, then do yourself a favor: Talk to your board members, interview them, investigate, ask questions, and write a profile on your lay leadership similar to the database fields suggested in chapter 8, exhibit 8.2. Our combined experience in talking to hundreds of nonprofits of all sorts and sizes leads us to believe that this exercise will produce information that, when acted upon, will produce networking opportunities an agency has never imagined. A word of advice, however— the agency's board must work in unison to achieve positive results. As the cliché goes, everyone must be on the same page. *Everyone* must be stakeholders. Doubters and naysayers should be rotated off the board. The size of the board member's gift should not be the first consideration—board members who are always giving criticism, most of which is not constructive, are usually people who cannot or will not add creative ideas to the building of a transformational team that will help the nonprofit build or rebuild its place in the community.

THE METAMORPHOSIS OF A TRANSFORMATIONAL DONOR

The dynamics of changing a transactional donor to a transformational donor-investor take place in the nonprofit's interaction with the potential donor investor. The transactional nature of the process is only a perception in the mind of the volunteer or professional staff member who has been asked to solicit this person. Many donors make a gift every year for a number of years without ever showing any inclination to become involved with the agency. The lay and professional leadership assume that the person is not interested in becoming active, or that, because of the person's prominence in the community, the gift itself was enough, thus taking the easy don't-rock-the-boat the way out.

Assumptions like this are often wrong. Perhaps this donor makes a higher than average annual gift. Why? Because he or she has an interest in the work of the nonprofit. A donor might give once to a nonprofit because a peer requests the gift as a favor, but a repeated, above-average annual gift is made only because the values of both the giver and the nonprofit are the same.

The reason the majority of donors do not get involved is that they are not asked. Cardinal Rule #1: You will not receive a gift if the prospective donor is not asked. This rule also applies to receiving an increased gift, or to metamorphosing a transactional donor into a transformational donor.

A personal, one-on-one meeting between solicitor and donor, sometimes also involving the nonprofit staff person assisting with the solicitation of the donor (in what is known as a *two-on-one meeting*) is the most successful way to build, rebuild, or stimulate the agency's fund-raising program. In addition to one-on-one or two-on-one meetings, the nonprofits receptions, special events, and any programs in which prospects meet with the agency's board members, lay leadership, current major givers, and staff all lead to a stewardship process that will help the agency attract donor-investors.

EXHIBIT 6.1 The High Impact Philanthropy Model: Balanced Partnership for Issues-Based Philanthropy

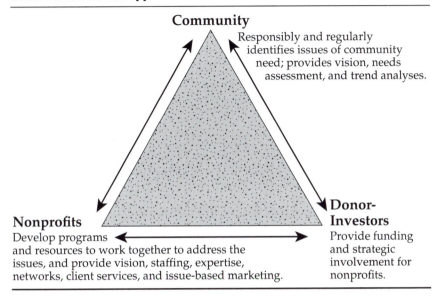

Community
Responsibly and regularly identifies issues of community need; provides vision, needs assessment, and trend analyses.

Nonprofits
Develop programs and resources to work together to address the issues, and provide vision, staffing, expertise, networks, client services, and issue-based marketing.

Donor-Investors
Provide funding and strategic involvement for nonprofits.

Most agencies take the path of least resistance: direct mail, phonathons, and other programs that distance the donor from the nonprofit. It is understandable that smaller agencies will concentrate on direct mail—but the cost in time and money is the factor the executive director must face. He or she may calculate that direct mail will bring in more money in a shorter period of time—that is, it will give more bang for the buck. Nevertheless, this is no way to build a constituency, and no way to add to the nonprofit's impact on the community it serves. (Direct mail has value as a donor acquisition vehicle, but all new donors need to be brought into a relationship with the nonprofit as soon as possible.)

CONCLUSION

The interaction among the community, the donor-investor and the nonprofit is best described as a quality-of-life relationship. We have described the interdependence of the nonprofit and the community in terms of which one benefits more from their mutual association; the answer is, of course, that both benefit, and to the same degree of satisfaction. We need to look at the philanthropic sector as a whole, an unbroken cyclical progression. The cycle begins with the definition of community needs, which are then expressed in the nonprofit's mission. The donor-investor becomes involved, and the cycle continually renews as these investors recruit others to become donor-investors.

The New Major Donors

Who They Are and What

They Are Looking For

Transformational giving is not a new phenomenon. Any study of nine-teenth- and twentieth-century philanthropy in America, and twentieth-century philanthropy in Europe, Canada, Latin America, Asia, and Australia, reveals a steady outpouring of gifts that have transformed com-munities and institutions. Although relatively few in number, and not widely publicized, they had a major impact. What most of these gifts had in common, relative to their origin, was that they came from traditional sources of philanthropic giving: wealthy families with a strong commit-ment to give back to the community, like Carnegie, Rockefeller, and Whit-ney; corporations like IBM, Bank of America, J. P. Morgan, American Express, and Burlington Northern; foundations such as Ford, David and Lucile Packard, and William and Flora Hewlett; and people who were gen-erally high-profile citizens or were from families with position and wealth.

In the late twentieth century, with its explosive science- and technol-ogy-driven economy and the intergenerational transfer of wealth, a new phenomenon emerged: nontraditional donors. They have joined, but not replaced, more traditional givers. Their gifts, in many cases, represent sig-nificant shifts from previous donor profiles. The way in which they want to be cultivated, solicited, and acknowledged is different, and they view their gifts more as investments than as donations. Their desire for involvement in the organizations in which they are investing is greater than that of most traditional donors and is, quite often, a point of concern or even anxiety for the recipient organization.

This outpouring of nonprofit community investment—the product of a robust economy and the heightened understanding by newly emergent financial and social leaders of the importance of philanthropy in address-ing issues, building communities, and creating sturdy institutions—is one of the most important milestones in the entire history of philanthropic growth. In the late twentieth century, and continuing in this new century, many major transformational gifts are coming from what has been termed the *new philanthropists.*

CHARACTERISTICS OF THE NEW PHILANTHROPISTS

Responsible for many transformational gifts, the new philanthropists have come from a number of new sources: the cyber and venture-capital rich; women; ethnic and racial groups previously underrepresented or under-recognized in philanthropy; and those who have become wealthy through the intergenerational transfer of trillions of dollars. These new philanthro-pists have exciting characteristics that promise to change the face of phi-lanthropy as well as the institutions and communities in which they have invested.

They may be young, middle-aged, or older, and they may come from a tradition of giving or from a culture and tradition where giving is new. They may seek institutions to fund, or they may invite funders to approach them. The varying coordinates provide a rich set of opportunities for or-ganizations that wish to cultivate and access these potential investors.

HOW THEY GIVE AND WHAT THEY EXPECT— SEVEN CHARACTERISTICS

Regardless of their age, experience, or tradition, these donors share some common characteristics. Primary research, through interviews and obser-vation, and secondary research from media coverage, have yielded these principal aspects of how they give and what they expect from nonprofits:

1. Their first gift is often a major gift—they may not grow through the giv-ing pyramid like traditional donors;
2. They invest in issues and expect results;
3. They seek values-driven organizations, often without realizing that it is the values that are attracting them;

4. They want organizations to accept their ideas and opinions, not just their money;

5. They are impatient for results;

6. They may be impatient for the ask;

7. They want to be involved, and often want a base of power or control in the program or organization.

Exploring How they Give and What They Expect

1. Their first gift is often a major gift-they may not grow through the giving pyramid like traditional donors. Because they want to make a difference, to have an impact, and to be able to see visible change, many of the new philanthropists begin by making a large gift. Traditional giving, in which nonprofits carefully track donors and gifts as they progress from initial to increased to special to major, seems too slow for many of the new philanthropists. Their issues orientation (see the following paragraph) motivates them to put substantial resources into a health or social problem so that it can be solved, or into a cultural or educational organization so that its work can flourish. Their first gift may be $10,000 or $100,000; they are more motivated by the issue and the urgency of that issue than by a need to grow gradually into a donor relationship. They often know what results they want and will ask what is needed to achieve those results. And, if it requires a major investment, they will make it.

2. They invest in issues and expect results. The September 1999 issue of *Wired* magazine carried an article entitled "Nonprofit Motive," the introduction of which read, "The new breed of Silicon Valley philanthropists would make Mother Teresa crunch the numbers. Call it virtue capital." Other Silicon Valley entrepreneurs, interviewed for the 1999 Annual Report of the Silicon Valley Community Foundation, stressed the importance of investing in change and seeing results. Further, those results are focused strongly on the issues the entrepreneurs are most concerned about including education, youth, and the environment. Cate Muther, a Silicon Valley entrepreneur who has started her own foundation, The Three Guineas (referencing Virginia Woolf's book of the same name), was questioned at a National Society of Fundraising Executives (NSFRE) meeting regarding the kinds of organizations to which she gives. She responded that she did not "give to organizations"—instead, she "gives to issues." Her issues include providing an incubator for women to get started in high-tech areas and to become involved in philanthropic pursuits. And, like so many new philanthropists, she identifies whom the foundation will fund. She does not accept solicitations. This trend in funding is a sea change from more traditional philanthropy, in which organizations relied on sentiment or a sense of duty to garner gifts from people who believed in the institution. Giving that is institution-focused—which Muther identified as her "community philanthropy" to her own university, her children's school, and other such organizations—is still popular and prevalent. However, for her foundation's investments, she looks for organizations that address the issues she has identified as critical to her vision and interests.

3. They seek values-driven organizations, often without realizing that it is the values that are attracting them.   Because they are issue-focused, new philanthropists are, implicitly, values-focused. Issues manifest values. The problem with many nonprofits is that they are hesitant to publicize their values. They mistakenly believe that the need to be businesslike and to have a solid business plan means that they cannot convey their values in their mission statement and materials. The quest for the "corporate mission statement" has so stripped some nonprofit materials of heart that they no longer convey appropriate messages to donors who are issues- and values-driven. Get your values out there. Weave them into your mission. Remember that for-profit advertising is almost entirely based on values (see Chapter 10). Our sector can honestly say it is driven by a values-based bottom line and it needs to gain much more confidence about revealing those values. The simplicity of some messages is inspiring: Stanford University Libraries, in a printed thank-you card to donors who had made gifts for a special conservation program, conveyed its values exquisitely: "Your gift to the Stanford University Libraries helps us assemble the sources, the arguments, the hypotheses, the wisdom and controversies of the ages. For all those here and those yet to come, please accept our gratitude." Signed by Michael Keller, the director of the University of Libraries, the librarian, this message conveyed the inherent values of a university library, along with thoughtful appreciation.

4. They want organizations to accept their ideas and opinions, not just their money.   Checkbook philanthropy is out; involvement is in. This is a problem for many organizations. Decades ago, when no one really understood (or perhaps needed to understand) the nonprofit sector and its organizations, there was a blissful distance between most donors and recipients. Donors who sat on boards were, of course, aware of the financial and values-based performance of the organizations they supported, but ongoing stewardship and involvement of other donor-investors was spotty and, to a large measure, not demanded by the donors. The new philanthropists do not want that distance. They want involvement. We are learning that those who create wealth, ideas, and companies are looking for opportunities to do more than observe. Younger philanthropists—or those with potential for philanthropy—often want hands-on experience volunteering for organizations. Through community foundations, and also through groups of young people who have formed "social venture" organizations, active volunteering takes place. The younger philanthropists paint clubhouses for teenagers, provide cars and drivers for the elderly, and find other community needs in which they can become involved. They also want to sit on boards. Organizations that are dismayed when large donors want a seat on their boards need to understand that this is a new era of philanthropy. It is not passive. It requires that the organization be open to letting the investor in. In one organization (an independent school), several donors to the library/media center—whose expertise and wealth grew out of the late twentieth-century technology achievements—were involved on the technology task force, traveled to visit other new library/media centers at other educational institutions to gather ideas, and signed off on the final schematic drawings for the building itself. There were frequent visits to the construction site, as the building was taking shape, and a continued involvement in the future of the school was assured. Their advice was sought and welcomed. Organizations should no longer equate this kind of giving with "buying a seat on the board"; this is a different kind of involvement and is sharply distinct from the passive board seat-holder. It is a distinguishing aspect of the new philanthropists, and one that needs to be addressed both at the policy level relative to board recruitment and composition and at the pragmatic level. While no organization wants a donor—even a transformational donor—to exert inappropriate control that exceeds or violates the mission, some organizations have policies and practices that deny these transforming donors access to the excitement their gift produces. A fear of accountability exists in far too many organizations to this day; If organizations are fearful of someone seeing the "inside" of their organization, then they are probably not ready for a transforming gift. Not all transformational donors want to be involved at the level described here; but when they do, organizations need to be ready to respond. Create a policy and enforce it, but don't pass up opportunities because you are fearful of the donor's scrutiny.

5. *They are impatient for results.*   The nonprofit sector is a paradox. It deals with urgent issues (education, health, welfare, culture, and the arts) with what seems, to some, as chronic slowness. Devoted to process and consensus, nonprofits seem unable to move swiftly enough for many of the new philanthropists. One donor complained that it had been "several months" since she had made her gift, and "nothing had happened." Non-

profits need to speed their processes and to be better communicators about the time it takes to develop and implement a program. Often, expectations are unrealistic. Conversations with new philanthropists—particularly those from the cyber and Internet worlds—reveal an often incredulous view of the time that it takes nonprofits to act. They regard even the smallest organizations as exceedingly bureaucratic and find, in particular, that the function of nonprofit boards relative to the decision-making of the organization is a mystery. Organizations must commit to a more nimble approach to implementation and communication when dealing with many of the new investments and donor-investors. The fault lies largely in doing things too slowly for the way the world is moving in the twenty-first century, but there are two other aspects as well. *First,* if the problem is so urgent that nonprofits seek transforming gifts to address it, then donors are hard-pressed to understand why the urgency with which the gift was solicited is not reflected in the urgency of the program, project, or building it will fund. *Second,* nonprofits that are devoted to process may not communicate effectively the steps they are taking in that process. Sometimes, on investigation, it turns out that the organization is moving forward but not successfully conveying its progress. These two points are compounded with another practice that needs changing: the tendency to communicate needs, not results.

6. *They may be impatient for the ask.* There is another aspect of the process orientation that feels too slow for some new major donors: the ask itself. The process that nonprofits have traditionally followed in soliciting gifts may not work with some of the new philanthropists. Cultivation and solicitation may be accelerated and may have an "on again, off again" pattern. Although personal connection is still elementary to successful transformational gifts, organizations frequently find themselves discussing the fine points of a gift via the Internet. Nonprofits need to adapt their processes to conform to the needs of each of these new donors, while taking care not to abandon good cultivation and solicitation procedures. More traditional givers will still be looking for a cultivation process; the newer philanthropists are often process-impatient and have been known to move on to other organizations that address the same issue, rather than wait for the first organization to get around to asking them. The approach to asking needs to change. Even more traditional donors who decide to make a transformational gift are increasingly impatient with the pace of the nonprofit sector and the bureaucracy of some institutions. Younger donors are very impatient, particularly those who have worked in high-tech, fast-paced companies. When they want information, they want it by e-mail or phone. They want transactions to take place at Internet speed. Accelerate the process if you need to. Internalize the steps and skip past those that don't seem necessary. And, if suggestions are made by donor-investors about speeding up processes or stripping out a few layers of bureaucracy, listen to them. These donors have known success because of their creation of wealth, their emergence into mainstream philanthropy, their climb up the corporate ladder, or their management of inherited wealth and their redirection of it into social ventures. The nonprofit sector can learn from these entrepreneurial thinkers.

7. They want to be involved, and often want a base of power or control in the program or the organization. A companion characteristic to the fourth point is the need these investors have to exercise power or control in the organizations in which they have made an investment. This is not just program involvement; this is the desire to be a decision-maker through board or key committee participation. Part of this is based on their own expertise and vision; another part has to do with what has been mentioned earlier: the difficulty many new philanthropists (and traditional philanthropists reflective the new economy) have with the way nonprofits conduct their business. They want a quantifiable return on their investment, which is very difficult for nonprofits to provide. It is the responsibility of nonprofits to educate their investors about the financial and values-oriented bottom lines of nonprofits, and how each can be measured. This requires a dedication and an ability to translate organizational activity into mission impact statements, while also equating actual results in a quantifiable manner. The nonprofit sector's reputation has been too often sullied by organizations that were recklessly casual about accountability. The 1980s and 1990s were heavily focused on redressing the "out of accountability" imbalance, but the diligence must persist. Philanthropists view their gifts—particularly transformational gifts—as investments. They want to know all dimensions of the return on that investment and will want to have an opportunity to influence outcomes. An effective nonprofit—one that can report with accuracy and evidence that, for example, their programs will save local, state, and federal agencies at least $6 million over 10 years—will see their investors' confidence increase. Until this confidence is established, those nonprofits that wish to attract transformational gifts—particularly from new philanthropists—may have to share some control with their investors by inviting them to sit on the board, be part of a committee or advisory board, or head up a task force in an area that relates to the implementation of their gift. These are the powerful ways in which they can be positively involved. Sitting in a seat of power when an investment has been made is the model with which the investors are most familiar. Nonprofits, in their partnership with the community and donor-investors, now need to invite them in to witness the impact of these gifts. All nonprofits, at some point, can benefit from investors who look critically and helpfully at our programs and practices.

WHAT THEY WILL DO AND WHAT THEY WANT

The new philanthropists offer what some more traditional philanthropists have not provided. These aspects of their giving are both pragmatic and idealistic; and the combination, when used to cement partnerships among nonprofits, communities, and these donors, can have high impact results.

Because they view nonprofits as catalysts to solve the problems they recognize in society, and because they are focused largely on issues rather than institutions, those new to philanthropy are willing to take risks and to try ideas that are a boon to nonprofits. This manifests itself in two key ways, which follow.

1. A Willingness to Make Longer Term Investments

This is an incredibly positive and important outgrowth of the venture capital industry. An article in the Harvard Business Review (1997) by Christine Letts, a lecturer at Harvard's John F. Kennedy School of Government, and two co-authors, William Ryan and Allen Grossman, addressed the differences in the ways nonprofits and private-sector businesses grow. In a series of seminars she conducted for fund raisers and business leaders in 1995 and 1996, Letts derived the thesis that venture capital practices—like helping management develop and execute strategies, measuring investment performance, and maintaining a long-term relationship—would help both funders and nonprofits. Letts found that in the five states with the most active foundation funders, only 5.2 percent of all grants were awarded for more than a year; in contrast, venture capitalists typically maintain relationships with companies for five years or more. Happily, this model is now being implemented in areas where venture capital influence is strong, and some new philanthropists are making three- to five-year commitments to nonprofits, some of which have high impact. One tiny organization (with a big educational mission) found itself the recipient of a three-year gift of $100,000 each year at a time when their entire budget was only $100,000 a year. A truly transforming gift like this requires that an organization determine how it will sustain itself as a $200,000+ per year organization, even after the grant money has been spent. This requires more vigorous management and fund-raising. Regarding the management assistance aspect of long-term investment, this, too, is happening. Technical assistance or capacity-building grants are granted with increasing favor. One organization that received multiyear funding for programs is now receiving, from the same funder, a grant to provide coaching and training for the highly talented and motivated individual in charge of a newly formed development program. This trend reveals another irony: The new philanthropists, and other transformational donors, want to make long-term investments, but they want short term results and an environment in which they are engaged and can savor the impact of their giving. Nonprofits need to recognize this irony and act on it.

2. A Desire to Transform Institutions and Society

Interviewed in the annual report of the Community Foundation Silicon Valley (1999), one young couple, Ray and Joanne Lin, expressed this idea: "We fund change, not charity." Like the Lins, many new philanthropists say that their giving has a single thrust, no matter what kind of organization they choose to fund; they want change. The change they seek is multifaceted: They want to change the circumstances that affect the issues they are interested in (e.g., leadership programs for girls or for particular ethnic or racial groups); they want to change the results of existing programs (e.g., schools); and they want to change philanthropy itself (e.g., through more active involvement, less passive giving). *Wired* magazine (www. wired.com, September 1999) points to the "new breed of high tech philanthropists" and says "they want to reinvent the art of generosity. They share [Infoseek founder Steve Kirsch's] sense that simply giving money away is too passive and uninvolved. They want to lend business expertise, identify and support 'social entrepreneurs' hungry to shake up the nonprofit world, and quantify their results. In short, they want to create a new kind of charity. But they don't call it that. They call it venture philanthropy." These venture philanthropists look for ways to get directly involved, and they decry what they call checkbook philanthropy as not enough.

WHAT NONPROFITS NEED TO KNOW ABOUT WHAT NEW PHILANTHROPISTS NEED

There are some other key concepts about the new philanthropists that expand our understanding of their philanthropic aspirations and needs.

First of all, *this isn't your father's philanthropy; it is more like your mother's. The giving/getting involved in the equation has shifted.* An interesting phenomenon of transformational giving, particularly from new philanthropists, is that it patterns the outcome of the studies done in women's philanthropy at the University of California at Los Angeles (UCLA) and the Women's Philanthropy Institute in Madison, Wisconsin. Andrea Kaminski, executive director of the Wisconsin organization, says, "Women, young or old, tend to want a hands-on approach and to be more involved with the program or project they start." Younger men and minority groups are also wanting more involvement, and this indicates that nonprofits and communities need to view their partnerships with donor-investors not in the passive "checkbook" philanthropic terms of decades past, but in the context of a model that requires more engagement. The research among women at UCLA revealed that they tend to get involved first, and make a financial commitment second. Traditional male donors, on the other hand, would often make a gift first and get involved later (typically, by sitting on the board). Today's philanthropists are getting involved—sometimes with an actual program or service—before making a significant commitment. Organizations need to provide opportunities for them to get involved and then to nurture the relationship in order to ensure its healthy and long-term growth. Because philanthropy is increasingly issues-oriented, organizations cannot rely on sentiment alone to maintain involvement. Although that may work for more traditional philanthropy (e.g., the alma mater, children's school, place of worship), it does not satisfy the donor's need to feel a sense of impact on an issue. If an individual is interested in the issue of diversity in private schools, for example, he or she can usually find a number of schools where this issue may be addressed. However, the one that will continue to receive investment is the one that both involves them and gives feedback based on results. Nonprofits, to maintain relationships successfully, need to keep focusing on issues and values.

Second, *if they are inexperienced with philanthropy but want to give, they also want to learn.* Nonprofits have a wonderful opportunity, in this golden age of philanthropy, to be teachers. This is particularly true in parts of the world where philanthropy is just emerging. Around the world, at the outset of the twenty-first century, there is a keen sense of the need to build community. We have seen devolution and the withdrawal of government from its funding role in many countries, including the United States. The Musée d'Art Asiatique (Guimet) in Paris is a splendid example of private funding infused into a national museum. A recent highly successful campaign for renovation of the museum centered its private funding efforts around the creation of a foundation (*foundation*) several years before the actual campaign began. The campaign, which drew both financial support and gifts to the collection from Europe and Asia, exceeded its goal. (See *International Fundraising*, Wiley, 1999, ed. Harris for examples of international development activities.) There is also a growing realization that nonprofit organizations can play a huge role in fortifying a community's ability to respond to change, meet needs, and provide programs and services at a cost that is significantly less than what government or private industry could provide. The link between community and nonprofits is strong: values. John W. Gardner, Haas Professor of Public Service at the Stanford Business School, believes that "communities are the ground-level generators and preservers of values and ethical systems" (Stanford Associates Report, 1982). Embracing the shared values basis of philanthropy, it is easy to see that an investment in a nonprofit is really an investment in the community (Grace, 1997). In this same article, Gardner stated that one of the ten ingredients of a sound and vital community is "a reasonable base of shared values . . . such as justice, equality, freedom, and so on." Nonprofits have the rare opportunity, with this new crop of philanthropically minded potential investors and an environment in which there is increased interest in community, to demonstrate that they are the vehicles for making the link between shared values and actions that will advance and maintain those values. In the marketing, outreach, and cultivation approaches that nonprofits undertake, they must be very aware of the incredible opporunity they have to educate—not only about their organization, but about the issue, the community, the shared values, and the way in which involvement in the organization (giving, asking, joining, serving) will build community.

Finally, *they are sometimes cautious with the initial gift, but they will make a really big investment if they see results or feel involved*. This is happening over and over, at universities, schools and in grassroots organizations. An initial major or annual investment leads to larger and larger gifts and greater and greater involvement. Early caution comes from lack of knowledge, lack of involvement and, sometimes with newly wealthy individuals, a lack of confidence about the giving process or whether they should be giving money away. Organizational sensitivity to new donor concerns is a key component of building a strong relationship. Nonprofits must not appear to be forcing a relationship or a request on an individual who is not ready to give initially or give more. Becoming a philanthropist, as a major donor, is a huge step for many people. Nonprofits must be perceived as there to guide, not to push.

CHALLENGES IN FINDING AND WORKING WITH NEW PHILANTHROPISTS

Among the many systems that are challenged by twenty-first-century philanthropy, few are more affected than research and the subsequent approaches to newly identified donors. Because of the focus on wealth and philanthropy in the media, few days pass without some profile of a newly wealthy individual or a person who has set aside a career in the corporate world after "cashing out" and is now devoting his or her life to nonprofit work.

Some areas of America and the world seem to incubate these millionaires of dot.com and venture capital successes, but parts of America and the world that are not spawning this wealth should not feel as though they cannot be part of the new era of philanthropy. They should look beyond their institutions and their locations to the power of their issue: As our global village shrinks and access to issues-based philanthropy grows, people who want to make a difference will seek investment opportunities around the world.

In a systematic approach to major gifts as a program, the new philanthropy presents some challenges in creating systems that will help organizations identify potential donors. Even for established colleges, universities, and schools—those with "natural constituencies"—there are new challenges in gathering information about young alumni who have no previous giving history and few known connections to the institution. Fortunately, technology and media coverage of successful young people and their philanthropy support the nonprofit's needs in this area. It is well to remember the following two things about managing a transformational giving program in this evolving era of philanthropy.

First of all, *the traditional grids, vectors, and sources don't work.* Many of these individuals are "below the radar." There is no *Who's Who* or other traditional sources to consult. They have little if any history of philanthropy, and tend not to be in the listings from other organizations. Standard research techniques have had to be modified; the Internet is the key for researching most of these individuals, and the data have to be woven together to create a profile. At Stanford University, Director of Research Randy Lakeman has constructed a thorough and effective program. Research has taken on a new dimension.

The second thing to remember is that *many new philanthropists want to seek institutions, not have institutions seek them.* Because of their issues focus, they look for organizations that have either a track record or great promise in addressing the areas of their greatest concern. Although an organization may identify an individual or foundation as a great match for their mission, it is inappropriate to self-identify when the funder has made clear that inquiries are not welcome. Marketing for fund and donor development has assumed a new importance in the environment of new philanthropy. Mission statements need to be focused on issues, not just organizations, and there needs to be public recognition for issue-based actions. An organization that provides low-cost housing for the working poor in a major city has received so much recognition for its low-overhead, client-centered housing and transition programs that they can hardly keep pace with the inquiries from potential funders. An annual event, involving high-profile community people, and the organization's integrity relative to the people served and the return on investment have catapulted this organization to a very admired (and envied) position. The media interest in the organization is keen, and investor satisfaction is high. Their strength comes from strong programming, an executive director whose passion for the mission is sincere and apparent and who is not timid about positioning the organization as a successful solution to a community problem, vigorous donor involvement, regular and accurate reporting of results, and the communication of the impact they are having on a widely understood problem in that city.

SOME SPECIAL ISSUES IN NEW PHILANTHROPY

Amidst the opportunities are some considerations of how to help these potential donors feel connected to organizations and to their communities. The age-old principle of the donor-centered world remains strong: Nonprofits need to seek these donors where they are, and respect who they are. Some considerations nonprofits may need to remember include the following:

- *The new philanthropists often don't "fit" with other donors; cultivation has to be tailored to their needs, preferences, and schedules.* Because of their youth, background, or lack of comfort with the traditional kind of philanthropic cultivation and recognition strategies, many of the new philanthropists shun "see and be seen" events, social lunches, large receptions, and general meetings. Forget black tie; they may not even own a regular tie. They prefer one-on-one meetings, e-mail dialogue, visits to and interaction with program staff, opportunities to review results and other experiences that relate more closely to their needs and interests.
- *They are making time for philanthropy; be respectful of that time because it is part of their gift.* Their schedules are often frenzied, and they may travel a great deal. One major donor has all of the principals from a major project he is funding on his e-mail "buddy list." It is not unusual for one of

the principals to receive a message from this donor while checking other e-mails: "Call me, I am in my office for the next 20 minutes," or "E-mail me—I need to know. . . ." Responding to donors or prospects in a way that is comfortable and appropriate for them has never been more important. In Silicon Valley, Seattle, Irvine, Boston, Austin, Colorado Springs, Neuilly (France), Kent (England), Singapore, and other places in America and the world where the influx of young people involved with high tech, bio tech and venture capital has been tremendous, the lessons learned by nonprofits are clear: Adapt to their style of communication and dress. Find out what their needs are and tailor programs to meet them. These are good lessons for all nonprofits, wherever they are.

- *The cyber- and venture-rich have formed many philanthropic organizations of their own, through which they may want to work and with which nonprofits need to form community partnerships.* This is one of the most intriguing aspects of the new philanthropy. The need to be involved and influence, coupled with impatience with existing institutions and the desire to direct their funds into issues of their own interest, has led to the formation of many new family foundations (the number has grown from 22,000 to 44,000 since 1980). Most notable, of course, is the Bill and Melinda Gates Foundation, into which the founders have put more than $22 billion. Nearly $2.3 million must be given now each day by the Gates Foundation to bring technology to issues of global health and education.

- *Opportunities to forge partnerships with community foundations abound, and nonprofits need to be seen as the "delivery system" for new programs of mutual interest to the donor and the community foundation.* Not every new fund or foundation is established as an independent entity. Community foundations in many communities have welcomed the opportunity to establish these funds as either donor-advised funds or supporting organizations. Using this model, entrepreneurs are able to leave the administration of the fund to an established community foundation while maintaining control over the disbursement of the funds. There are other approaches as well. One of the most visible Internet companies, eBay, set aside more than 100,000 shares of their pre-IPO stock to create the eBay Foundation. In 1998, the fund had grown to $30 million, and the founders were beginning to make community investments. Today, the fund has grown substantially and its example has encouraged others to begin foundations using pre-IPO stock.

- *Connection with venture capital funds can benefit donors, communities, and nonprofits.* In other cases, venture capital firms have established funds by inviting the companies they fund to put stock options into a venture fund that is then disbursed to nonprofits in their communities. Gib Meyers of the Mayfield Fund in Menlo Park, California, has created the Entrepreneurs' Foundation, a venture philanthropy group. Meyers and other members of the Entrepreneurs' Foundation are, according to *Wired* magazine (September 1999), coming up "with novel ways to track the effectiveness of their donations, much as they track their ROIs [return on investments]. The Entrepreneurs' Foundation also seeks to get its member companies engaged in (community) projects. . . ." The article continues, "Crucial to Venture Philanthropy 101 are the same financial instruments that build personal fortunes in high tech: stock options and IPOs. It's relatively painless for paper millionaires to give away shares . . . and pre-public companies can afford to be generous with options, too. . . . Meyers has wrung about $100,000 each in stock options from 36 companies." In September 1999 the Entrepreneurs' Fund had risen to an estimated $3.5 million. This phenomenon need not be viewed as something that can only happen through a venture capital firm. These models can work anywhere. One university in a fast-growing community is exploring how to set up its own venture fund through involvement of the young people who are pouring into that community and have no social or volunteer involvement. They plan to position the university as a resource for making connections, friends, and a difference.

- *Business and civic leaders who represent philanthropically emergent ethnic and racial groups have formed organizations that are increasingly interested in supporting issues through nonprofits.* Hispanic and Asian-American Chambers of Commerce in many communities, as well as organizations like Hispanics in Philanthropy (HIP) and 100 Black Men, are taking an active role in providing financial support and board members for organizations. As part of the new philanthropy, these groups are tremendous resources for organizations that recognize the importance of involving diverse leadership and philanthropic groups in their activities.

THE NEW PHILANTHROPISTS: FOOTHOLD IN THE FUTURE

On Friday, February 11, 2000 the *New York Times* ran a front page article entitled "Internet's Fortune Makers Giving It Away, Their Way." Many of the observations echo those of this chapter. However, the article adds a few critical points.

- The new philanthropists don't like the word "philanthropy." They find it very off-putting. Paul Shoemaker, director of Social Venture Partners, a Seattle network of 236 members mostly from the high-tech field, says that the term philanthropy "has sort of this blue-blooded connotation to it." Terms more in vogue are "social investment," "venture philanthropy," and "giving back to the community." (This author would add another word to the list of those to retire: "charity." It denotes another era and fails to convey the vigor and impact of the nonprofit sector.)

- While the economic boom may be a short-term phenomenon, the long-term benefit of the wealth and philanthropic vehicles created during this boom will linger and be part of the social fabric of America and the world (the Gates Foundation is global in its impact). As an example, the assets of the Community Foundation Silicon Valley have grown 25 to 40 percent in each of the years from 1997 through 1999, and contributions were expected to double in 2000. The Foundation now administers 675 different philanthropic funds that have been established by "living, breathing donors," most of which are tied to high tech in some way.

- Nicholas Lovejoy, one of the original founders of Amazon.com, began and ended the *Times* article. His final comment closes this chapter: "I'm absolutely convinced I can do anything that other people think is impossible, because we did it regularly at Amazon. We did the impossible on a regular basis, and that's a great experience to live through. And that's simply the attitude I want to apply to what we're trying to do now." Lovejoy and his wife, Barbara Gordon, run the Gordon-Lovejoy Foundation, which supports conservation demonstration projects. Thus far, they have given away $120,000 drawn from assets of $2.5 million. They are "thinking hard" about how best to use not just their unexpected wealth, but also their talents and time.

As nonprofit managers and volunteers, and for those with wealth that they want to invest, that is the key question.

8 ▼ Identifying the Transformational Giver

Most major gift scenarios begin after the executive director (ED) has received a telephone call from a board member, who has told the ED to rush to get in touch with the community's leading philanthropist because the board member happens to know that another nonprofit is about to approach the philanthropist for a very major gift.

As the scenario unfolds, the ED frantically calls every senior member of the board and/or the executive committee to find someone who knows him personally, and who will make an appointment for the ED and the board member to meet with him before the competing nonprofit can get to him. All thought of doing basic research is forgotten in the haste to make an appointment and ask for money from someone who, for all the ED and the board member know, may not be interested in the work of the nonprofit. If they are fortunate, the philanthropist may have made a token gift of $100 to one of the agency's special-event dinners, so he will at least know the name of the nonprofit. However, the dinner was probably the last time he has even thought of the organization or what it was about; but, having attended a fund raiser put on by the nonprofit, the philanthropist agrees to see his friend on the board and the ED.

Being a prominent citizen, and very wealthy, he has a good idea why these people are visiting him—and it isn't for the view from his fiftieth-floor office. He knows what's coming but is too polite to give his friend and the ED the brush-off over the telephone. Besides, he is curious about the sudden interest he's been receiving from nonprofits like this one, nonprofits to which he has never made a substantial gift or shown any interest.

The ED and the board member arrive at the designated time and are ushered into his office, which is sumptuous and full of original modern art, with an incredible a view, as rumor has suggested. Refreshments are offered, small talk is made until it seems one or the other speaker has run out of interesting chit-chat, and the conversation must be led to the subject at hand. Before leaving for this meeting, the nonprofit team agreed that the ED would begin the conversation with an overview of the nonprofit's work, emphasizing the agency's value to the community. At an appropriate time the ED will pause, and the board member will take over, telling a brief story about a particular program in which he or she is especially interested—one whose unique outcome (the board member believes) will interest the philanthropist. While the board member is talking, any of the following may take place:

1. The philanthropist begins to listen more intently when his peer describes the agency program that has interested him personally, in which he has become actively involved in giving time, advice, and support. Now he remembers why he made that gift at the agency's last special event. His motivation was:
   a. His parents or grandparents had used its senior services.
   b. The mayor or a member of the board of supervisors had told him about the good work the agency was doing with
      i. The homeless.
      ii. The struggle against AIDS.
      iii. Job retraining programs.
      iv. Hundreds of other programs that help people.
2. The philanthropist interrupts and preempts the solicitation by offering to give a gift in the lower quadrant of the amount the nonprofit team planned to ask for.
3. He sits there with an enigmatic look on his face, giving the impression that he will never enter into this discussion no matter how hard they try to engage him.
4. He starts looking at his wristwatch, giving a not-so-subtle hint that he has better things to do.

No matter how the solicitors feel about the philanthropist's response, they may take the proffered gift, stammer, and let him get the better of them with his silence. Or they may blurt out an amount prematurely and finish by walking away with a check—a substantial one compared to those he has written in past years—but with thousands of future dollars and potential support left behind on the table. Why? Because this has not been a transformational solicitation—it has been a *transaction*.

The solicitation team was not prepared. They reacted on a rumor and on the unsophisticated lack of knowledge of a well meaning lay leader. *Research* should have been their the key word. Without it, this nonprofit and thousands like it will fail to thrive while other agencies bask in the light of financial success. This is what this chapter is all about: linking the donor-investor to the nonprofit organization to the community. Research will identify the potential donor-investor's values and interests. Linking the potential donor-investor to the nonprofit via the process of transformational support will lead to high impact philanthropy, the support that every community is looking for.

WHO ARE THESE PEOPLE, AND WHAT MAKES THEM DONATE (OR NOT DONATE)?

A December 20, 1998, article in the *New York Times,* "How the Other Half Gives" by Geraldine Fabrikant and Shelby White, delves into the giving habits of twelve high-powered (but not always high-profile) executives from the nation's 500 biggest companies. The interview questions went further than merely how much these people gave to charity; they also asked about motivation, philosophy of giving, and who were the recipients of this philanthropy. These last three categories are of interest to our discussion on transformational giving and high impact philanthropy. Eight of the twelve executives made their large gifts through private foundations. Of the remaining four, all made gifts from their personal assets, and only one of these definitely stated that he or she did not establish a private foundation. At least eleven executives' giving patterns mirrored the giving profiles of their corporations. For example, one chairman gave $100 million to a university medical school, and his corporation also made a substantial gift to the same medical school. This person also gave a large gift to an arts organization. The arts organization named a building, and the medical school named both a building and the entire school after the donor and his wife. What makes this person's charitable gifts unique is that he is also the chairman of both institutions' boards of directors. He is the perfect example of a transformational giver who has made an impact on the community through his high impact philanthropy—his financial support, his time, and his energy!

After reading about the philanthropists in the *Times* article, many readers may ask themselves, "Why aren't these leaders active with our nonprofit organization?" They aren't active and don't give because they haven't been asked—because these organizations don't know them, don't know their values, and have not completed the basic research that would lead to a contact with them.

Not all nonprofits have missions and visions that will appeal to the major-donor investors described in the article; our society is layered with large organizations usually pictured at the top of the philanthropic pyramid, with the other agencies somewhere beneath them. This does not mean that the nonprofits below the peak are any less important or that they have only minor values to give to their communities. By definition, all nonprofits are agents of social change; they may vary in size, but not in impact on the community. Just as there is a variety of nonprofit organizations, however, there is also a variety of donor-investors with differing levels of wealth that they can donate to the nonprofit agencies that share their values. The lay leader or member of the professional staff of a nonprofit should not get depressed when reading of the mega-investors and their gifts. Agency leaders should instead think of what the organization can achieve with the local millionaire(s) instead of stewing about the billionaire whose ego requires his name on the building. Most nonprofit organizations will not receive gifts from mega-donors but are more likely to benefit from gifts made by donors who have the capacity to give in the area of $1 million. There are more potential givers capable of giving in this neighborhood, and access to these givers can usually be had through networking with the agency's own board of directors (as described later in this chapter).

If your community actually is home to a billionaire, remember that he or she will also donate to a smaller nonprofit if their values are mutual and the nonprofit has a program that will achieve those values. The techniques we describe can be applied to all donor-investors regardless of how much wealth they have. High impact philanthropy does not discriminate—one donor's thousands can achieve quality results in the community just as well as the other donor's millions. It's simply a matter of scale.

CHARACTERISTICS OF THE DONOR INVESTOR

What characteristics are shared by donors of major gifts? Thomas Stanley, in *The Millionaire Mind* (Andrews McMeel, 2000) makes the point that the majority of millionaires are not ostentatious spenders whose lifestyles are at the cutting edge. To the contrary, they live what many would describe as elegant, low-key lives involved in and enjoying what their communities offer, and making contributions through their interests in the arts and social causes. In an interview in *Modern Maturity*.[1] Stanley says that "You can't be at Saks and raising money for charity at the same time. And 64 percent of these people are involved in fundraising, 68 percent in community and civic activities."

[1] Interview by Susan Garland, *Modern Maturity* 43 (4): 43-45.

Can a certain trend be deduced from the executives' giving habits as described in the *Times* article (p. 103)? It's obvious that the donor-investor who can control the philanthropic purse strings of his or her corporation can achieve the ultimate in transformational giving. The examples were 12 executives of large corporations; however, this same paradigm, as we have explained, can also apply to executives of small to medium-sized companies.

Major gift donors are not restricted to people over the age of 50! The traditional middle-aged millionaire with inherited assets (or assets built up over decades) has been joined by the now generation, ranging in age from 25 up. The new millionaires—many of them from the dot.com world—are more interested in creativity and in using their money to lead the way to new social paradigms. Their involvement with nonprofits follows along these lines. They want to be actively involved with the nonprofits, to give of their expertise and management skills. Many of these new millionaires' role models were their parents. The largest givers over the past few years have been Bill and Melinda Gates. Bill Gates' parents were actively involved with many nonprofits in Seattle, Washington. These major-donors do not involve themselves with every nonprofit they fund; they know what areas of the nonprofit world they want to support, and with elaborate research on each nonprofit's mission and programs, make an impact on the community in a very direct way.

HOW TO ACHIEVE SUCCESSFUL RESULTS

Two things must be determined before you walk into a meeting with a donor. First, you must ask yourself the following questions: Has the case for the nonprofit been made? Is your prospect aware of the work of the nonprofit? Does your nonprofit's mission match the interests of the donor? Without answers to all these questions, the potential gift may be left ungiven. Second, you must know the financial background of your prospect. For example, is your prospect really wealthy enough to make a major gift according to your organization's definition of a major donation, or is he or she simply talented at stretching a modest income so well that it appears to be more than it is? A thorough job of research will avoid embarrassment for both the prospect and the nonprofit agency—and yes, the nonprofit does care about embarrassing the prospect because the future might change for this person, and the nonprofit agency could, by acting responsibly, be a recipient of his or her newfound largesse.

Research can be the easiest task; as we will discuss later in this chapter, many techniques can be used to determine whether a person has the capacity to make a major contribution to the nonprofit. The larger problem is actually recruiting the prospect into the agency's culture, which means finding the key that will turn the prospect into a major giver and an investor in the nonprofit. (Chapter 7 describes in detail various keys that can change the transactional giver into a transformational giver.) Before searching for that key, we have to classify the potential donor as to yearly cash compensation, total compensation, and how he or she contributes (or if he or she contributes at all) to nonprofits that interest him or her. The remainder of this chapter will show you how to locate the mission-driven donor who can become both a transformational giver and a potential board member.

THE NETWORK MAP

To assist the nonprofit lay leader you must learn to construct a network map. This map is built on the information in the agency's database: current donors, donors who have given during the past three to five years, and other prospects selected by the nonprofit's leadership and executive staff for potential stewardship. Use a spreadsheet that can be easily managed by a member of your support staff, and be sure it includes the following fields:

- First name
- Last name
- Middle initial
- Residence address
- Business address
- Telephone numbers: home, office, cellular, and pager (one field for each)
- E-mail address
- Web site URL
- Place of birth
- Birthdate
- Parents' names
- Spouse's and children's names
- High school
- College
- University
- Fraternal and club memberships
- Profession
- Professional associations

- For-profit and not-for-profit board memberships
- Outstanding achievements (inventions, books authored, public offices held, military awards, and awards by professional and nonprofit organizations)
- Names of close friends
- Affiliations with other nonprofits
- Comments (a field to keep track of the meetings with the donor/prospect)

Obviously, not every piece of information will be available for every prospect; but each profile will have the basic information that will allow some members of your board to link up with the prospect. Note that we have included even the high school the prospect attended. This information is very important in communities where many people tend to go to private high schools and keep strong ties to their schools through alumni groups. This is also the situation with some public high schools (e.g., Bronx High School of Science in New York and Lowell in San Francisco). When one or more map points coincide with those of a board member or a current major giver, you and that individual can discuss the strategy for approaching a prospect. (At this point the cliché about no one being more than six generations or friendships away from anyone else in the world begins to seem very real.) Remember, this is not like the usual transactional solicitation, in which you arrange a meeting and present the agency to the prospect. This is a request for a transformational gift—a gift that will have an impact on the agency and the community. It is an investment in the agency's current and future work, an investment that can be made many times during the year.

This network map is often referred to as a *demographic database*. If possible, you should add one other piece of information to it. This information is harder to obtain, but worth all of the trouble and time needed to collect it. It is referred to as a *psychobiography,* or a psychographic study of the potential prospect. This study can help answer the following questions and will help your organization find donors who can bring high impact philanthropy to your agency. The study helps you determine whether the prospect:

- Cares about the issues
- Wants change
- Wants to give back to the community where he or she grew wealthy
- Wants to guarantee the values to which he or she adheres are continued in the community
- Desires family-name recognition, whether associated with a program or on a bricks-and-mortar building

EXHIBIT 8.1 Psychobiographic Survey

1. Are you affiliated in any way with [name of your agency]?   Yes   No
   If yes, for how long? _____

2. What is the largest amount you have donated to any nonprofit? _____

3. What is the approximate total of yearly gifts you donate to all nonprofits? _____

4. How do you determine the amount to give each nonprofit?
   _____ Percentage of annual income
   _____ No set formula
   _____ Other

5. Please check each of your nonprofit interests:
   _____ Education
   _____ Health
   _____ Social issues
   _____ Environment
   _____ Religion
   _____ The Arts

6. What do you consider to be your most important personal concern?
   _____
   _____

7. How have you learned about the nonprofits to which you currently contribute?
   _____ From lay leaders
   _____ Media sources
   _____ Other

The above survey is the most efficient way to get the answers to the questions on the previous page. Ideally, the potential prospect should answer it, but that can be difficult if your agency links with the person are superficial (he or she is known only as an acquaintance of a board member or other lay leader). If you are fortunate enough that a member of the committee is a close friend of the prospect and can answer these questions, then the development committee is starting out well ahead and can work with the prospect's appointment team and make a list of appropriate questions to ask.

RESEARCH TECHNIQUES AND RESOURCES

Remember, research will give you only the financial and a few stark personal facts about potential donors—their capacities to give, not their motivations. Too many times we have seen development committee members blanch (figuratively speaking) when they find out how wealthy one of their non–donor investor peers is; the next question out of their mouths is usually, "Why doesn't this person give any money [or so little money] to our agency?" The reasons may be many and usually are hidden in the mind of the prospect. Research can provide facts—but not reasons.

To obtain new donor-investors you start with names—but where do these names come from? The first source is the board of directors of your agency, whose members by now think they have probably yielded all the names they have to give. So what is the next source? Local and regional newspapers can be excellent places to find names of potential donor-investors, in the society columns, the business pages, and even the general news sections. The people written about often have money, clout, and a desire to do good. They like to see their names in the newspapers and hear them talked about on the radio and television, especially in association with a worthy nonprofit. Look in local society, gossip and business sections and the various regional issues of the *Business Times. Fortune* and *Forbes* also publish yearly lists of the top corporations in the United States, including salary information on the top executives. If your development staff works with very prominent prospects, we recommend you subscribe regularly to either the *New York Times, Wall Street Journal, Washington Post, Los Angeles Times,* or other metropolitan newspaper.

The Internet is another excellent resource for names and facts. Through the Securities and Exchange Commission's (SEC's) web site (http://www.sec.gov) you can view corporate proxy statements, which contain a wealth of information about the financial affairs of the board members and corporate officers. A proxy statement gives a short biography of each member of the board of directors and tells how many shares of the corporation's stock and how many options he or she owns. If your prospect is one of the officers of a listed corporation, the proxy is a good way to research the prospect's annual compensation, bonuses, allowances, stock awards, and other compensation details.

A prospect's personal or professional web site can give the researcher valuable historical information to help fill out the psychobiography survey. Such web sites are very useful when the prospect is a member of a private corporation or partnership that does not have to report information to the government.

Libraries, in addition to providing access to newspapers and the Internet, contain many volumes that can in their own right prove invaluable for research. Books include *Who's Who in America* and *Who's Who in Business and Finance,* both of which are good resources for background information.

REVERSE NETWORKING

Reverse networking refines the selection process by narrowing the field to those the board of directors, the development committee, and the executive and development directors believe would respond positively to a meeting with a peer, a board member, or both (Wendroff 1999).

How does this refinement of the process differ from any other solicitation approach? Normally, committees assemble lists of everyone of wealth in the community, then plan elaborate strategies to solicit these people. If any research is done, it is minimal; most candidates are not personally known by anyone connected with the organization. The results are usually below expectations, and the board and the development committee quickly becomes disenchanted with the project. This is the shotgun approach to solicitation.

Reverse networking, on the other hand, produces a selective list of prospects using research and community knowledge. From a large list of prospects the board and development committee pick and choose those people with whom they have personal contacts, or those with whom other individuals in the nonprofit can help make appointments (in which the chance for success is much greater than with the practice of cold calling).

Other Techniques

In addition to doing your own research using the previously mentioned sources you can also hire private research companies that will produce names of people of wealth along with short profiles of their business, personal, and professional activities. These companies can find information on almost every corporation listed and traded on the stock market and on their boards of directors. They can also obtain information on private corporations that have sold bonds to the public or have contracted with a federal agency.

For the nonprofit whose small staff has enough to do without spending days researching corporations from the SEC database, these private research companies are a godsend—but they don't come cheap. Your agency will have to pay, perhaps quite a bit, for this information. In exchange, your nonprofit will receive much of the information that can be entered into the fields

EXHIBIT 8.2   Securities Holding Research

T. F. Wealth ID Securities MATCH ™

22-May-00   Demonstration Data

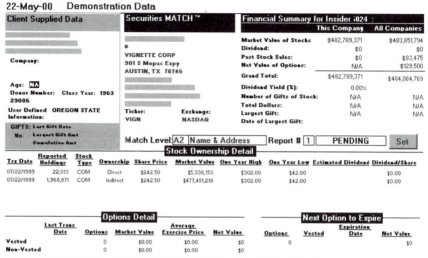

Client Supplied Data	Securities MATCH™	Financial Summary for Insider i024 :		
			This Company	All Companies
	B	Market Value of Stocks	$482,789,371	$483,851,794
	VIGNETTE CORP	Dividend:	$0	$0
Company:	901 S Mopac Expy	Past Stock Sales:	$0	$83,475
	AUSTIN, TX 78746	Net Value of Options:	N/A	$129,500
Age: **N/A**		Grand Total:	$482,789,371	$484,064,769
Donor Number: Class Year: 1963		Dividend Yield (%):	0.00%	
29086		Number of Gifts of Stock:	N/A	N/A
User Defined OREGON STATE	Ticker: Exchange:	Total Dollars:	N/A	N/A
Information:	VIGN NASDAQ	Largest Gift:	N/A	N/A
GIFTS: Last Gift Date		Date of Largest Gift:		
No. Largest Gift Amt				
Cumulative Amt				

Match Level: A2 | Name & Address   Report # 1   **PENDING**   Set

Stock Ownership Detail

Trx Date	Reported Holdings	Stock Type	Ownership	Share Price	Market Value	One Year High	One Year Low	Estimated Dividend	Dividend/Share
07/22/1999	22,013	COM	Direct	$242.50	$5,338,153	$302.00	$42.00		$0.00
07/22/1999	1,968,871	COM	Indirect	$242.50	$477,451,218	$302.00	$42.00		$0.00

Options Detail

	Last Trans Date	Options	Market Value	Average Exercise Price	Net Value
Vested		0	$0.00	$0.00	$0
Non-Vested		0	$0.00	$0.00	$0

Next Option to Expire

	Options	Vested	Expiration Date	Net Value
	0			$0

outlined on page 106, as well as financial information on the prospect's total known assets, the market value of his or her public stocks, and the market value of his or her residential properties (see exhibits 8.2–8.5).

Having spent the funds and received the information from the private research company, you may be unsure of how to use it. Your agency wouldn't be the first—how many times have nonprofits spent funds to purchase equipment, software, and information that has gathered dust on the shelf? Probably far too many times.

Therefore, you spend money on private research, spend a few dollars on organizing a meeting between the board and advisory lay leaders (who will be using this information) and the prospective donor-investors. The purpose of organizing this committee is to match up your lay leaders with the prospects. Matching up means that prospect A is a friend of board or advisory member B, or B knows someone at A's corporation who can and is willing to make an introduction to A on behalf of the nonprofit agency. This is the first strategy meeting, the first step in guiding the prospect along the path to becoming a transformational donor-investor. *This is not a solicitation meeting.* Don't blow it by asking for a gift. If, after or during the meeting, a gift is offered, accept it with grace—don't even look at the amount until you are out of the prospect's office or home. A very sincere thank you is all that is required at this time.

EXHIBIT 8.3 Executive Report

		Executive Report
ID Number:		May 22, 2000

CLIENT-SUPPLIED DATA

Individual

Business

Gifts

Last Gift Date:
Largest Gift Amount:
Cumulative Amount:
Number of Gifts:

User Defined 1	OREGON STATE
User Defined 2	
Class Year:	1963
Age:	

BIOGRAPHICAL INFORMATION

Spouse Name:		Birthdate:	09/29/1958
Spouse Birthdate:	12/20/1958	Minor Children:	Unknown

FINANCIAL SUMMARY — All Companies and Properties   **NEXT OPTION TO EXPIRE**

Market Value of Stocks:		$93,940,051		
Estimated Market Value of Properties	$851,000	-	$900,000	Company:
Net Value of Options:		$86,876		Shares:
Past Stock Sales:		$83,475		Possible Net Gain:
Estimated Annual Dividends:		$0		Expiration Date:
Grand Total of Known Assets:	$94,961,402	-	$95,010,402	

Company:	TYLAN GENERAL INC
Shares:	5000
Possible Net Gain:	$43,750
Expiration Date:	05/25/1/

SECURITIES CHANGE DETAIL

	(05/00) Current	(03/00) Previous	Dollar Change	Percent Change
Total Market Value:	$93,940,051	$483,851,794	($389,911,743)	-80.58
Total Dividend:	$0	$0	$0	0.00
Total Past Stock Sales:	$83,475	$83,475	$0	0.00
Total Net Value of Options:	$86,876	$129,500	($42,624)	-32.91
Total All Companies:	$94,110,402	$484,064,769	($389,954,367)	-80.56

SECURITIES MATCH SUMMARY

Insider Name	Insider Title	Company Name	Ticker	Company Total	Report #
	B	VIGNETTE CORP	VIGN	$482,789,371	1
	D	PSINET INC	PSIX	$1,148,173	1
	B	CASCADE COMMUNICATIONS COR	D.CSCC	$83,475	1
	SH	TYLAN GENERAL INC	TYGN	$43,750	1
	D	WORLDTALK COMMUNICATIONS C	WTLK	$0	1
	B	SUPERMAC TECHNOLOGY INC	SMAC	$0	1
	B	INTERNATIONAL NETWORK SERVIC	INSS	$0	1
	B	ATRIA SOFTWARE INC	ATSW	$0	1

REAL ESTATE MATCH SUMMARY   In Thousands

Match Name	Address	Value	Lower	Upper	Zip Median	Assessed	Purchase
		$854	$851	$900	$346	$901	$830

NET WORTH RESULT

Net Worth Code	5	Value Range:	$1 Million+	.

Copyright 2000, Thomson Financial. Used with permission.

EXHIBIT 8.4 Networking Report

			Individual Networking Report	
ID Number:			**May 22, 2000**	

CORPORATE

Company Name Address	Insider Name	Insider Title	Company Total	Report #
CASCADE COMMUNICATIONS CORP				
WESTFORD, MA 01886	SMITH DANIEL E	CEO, D, P	$101,255,738	2
PSINET INC				
HERNDON, VA 20170	COPELAND MARY KAY		$0	1
VIGNETTE CORP				
AUSTIN, TX 78746	DUFFIELD DAVID A		$0	2
	TAYLOR MARGARET L		$0	1

INDUSTRY (Companies with unspecified industries are not included)

Industry Companies in this Industry	Affiliated Insiders	Company Total	Report
Communica Tech			
ASCEND COMMUNICATIONS INC	SMITH DANIEL	$23,699,643.00	2
	SMITH DANIEL E	$2,703,975.00	2
CASCADE COMMUNICATIONS CORP		$101,255,738.00	2
OPENROUTE NETWORKS INC		$407,500.00	2
Ind/Com Svc			
AMERICA SERVICE GROUP INC	WRIGHT RICHARD D	$25,788.00	1
CELERIS CORP	TECKMAN DAVID R	$45,000.00	2
CLAREMONT TECHNOLOGY GROUP INC	TAYLOR MARGARET L	$0.00	1
LABORATORY CORP OF AMERICA HLDS INC	SMITH BRADFORD T	$682,522.00	2
PSINET INC	COPELAND MARY KAY	$0.00	1
VERIO INC	DUFFIELD DAVID A	$0.00	2
	TAYLOR MARGARET L	$0.00	1
Software			
CADENCE DESIGN SYSTEMS INC	WRIGHT JOHN P	$798,455.00	2
EBIX COM INC	DYER JAYE F	$0.00	2
FAIR ISAAC & CO INC	TAYLOR MARGARET L	$15,000.00	1
INFOSEEK CORP	WRIGHT LESLIE E	$0.00	1
KEANE INC	RUETTGERS MICHAEL	$1,001,124.00	1
MEDICALOGIC INC	TAYLOR RONALD R	$10,470,089.00	2
NICHOLS RESEARCH CORP	HASE RAYMOND C JR	$0.00	1
PEOPLESOFT INC	DUFFIELD CHERYL D	$156,659,487.00	1
	DUFFIELD DAVID A	$2,110,643,268.00	1
	TAYLOR MARGARET L	$105,770,735.00	1
	ZEIFANG AMY	$0.00	2
QAD INC	EGGERDING CHARLES	$0.00	1
VIGNETTE CORP	DUFFIELD DAVID A	$0.00	2
	TAYLOR MARGARET L	$0.00	1
VITRIA TECHNOLOGY INC	YOUNGER WILLIAM H	$306,832,543.00	2

GEOGRAPHIC

Zip	ID	Client-Supplied Name	City	State	Total all Companies	Report #
94025 E762		JANE E. CARPENTER	ATHERTON	CA	$3,195,235	1

EXHIBIT 8.5 Real Estate Watch

T. F. Wealth ID Real Estate MATCH™

22-May-00   Demonstration Data

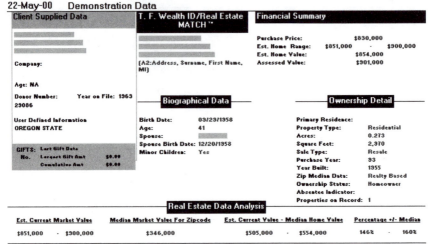

Client Supplied Data	T. F. Wealth ID/Real Estate MATCH™	Financial Summary		
		Purchase Price:	$830,000	
		Est. Home Range:	$851,000	$900,000
		Est. Home Value:	$854,000	
Company:	(A2:Address, Surname, First Name, MI)	Assessed Value:	$901,000	
Age: NA				
Donor Number: Year on File: 1963	**Biographical Data**		**Ownership Detail**	
29086				
User Defined Information	Birth Date: 03/29/1958	Primary Residence:		
OREGON STATE	Age: 41	Property Type:	Residential	
	Spouse:	Acres:	0.273	
	Spouse Birth Date: 12/20/1958	Square Feet:	2,970	
GIFTS: Last Gift Date	Minor Children: Yes	Sale Type:	Resale	
No. Largest Gift Amt $0.00		Purchase Year:	93	
Cumulative Amt $0.00		Year Built:	1955	
		Zip Median Data:	Realty Based	
		Ownership Status:	Homeowner	
		Absentee Indicator:		
		Properties on Record:	1	

Real Estate Data Analysis			
Est. Current Market Value	Median Market Value For Zipcode	Est. Current Value - Median Home Value	Percentage +/- Median
$851,000 - $900,000	$346,000	$505,000 - $554,000	146% - 160%

PROFILE OF A DONOR-INVESTOR

The model donor-investor is a person concerned with bringing personal values to the community through the nonprofit agency that best expresses those values through its programs.

What are those value concepts? Integrity, truth, worth, merit, goodness, excellence, and caliber are a few that the donor-investor considers before making a major gift and affiliating with the organization. Whether the donor-investor is interested in health, education, welfare, the arts, religion, or human relations, he or she wants to transfer these values to a program that benefits the community.

When does the donor-investor make this transformational gift? When she is convinced that the nonprofit agency meets her standards for investment (i.e., the nonprofit operates in a manner that the donor-investor can be proud of) and that the organization's reputation in the community for achieving its goals is recognized.

The donor-investor may make the major gift to the general fund of the agency if she knows the nonprofit is fiscally responsible. The donor can designate the funds for a specific program, piece of equipment, or building (or part of one) or to an endowment fund where the income will fund a particular project.

The major gift is made because the loop is completed and the donor-investor has become a true transformational giver.

CONCLUSION

Finding, identifying, and recruiting the donor-investor, then leading that person to the transformational giving level, is the goal of this book and this chapter. The result will be high impact philanthropy. The process and procedures to accomplish these goals have been explained and illustrated so that there are no doubts about what to do or, how to do it.

The technique of reverse networking will bring a higher percentage of success than using a less systematic method. Doing your research on the prospect will give you information that ensures a better than 50 percent chance of recruiting him or her for your agency. Research can also show that a potential prospect is not for your nonprofit. There are many reasons, but the main one is that the prospect is already heavily involved with an agency that serves your community in the same manner yours does. If a member of your board has a close tie to this person, make the effort to meet with him or her. There may be reasons no one knows about that will change this person's perspective, and your meeting might just be the catalyst that could recruit the person to your agency—if not now, maybe in the near future.

PART III

THE NEW DONOR/ORGANIZATION PARTNERSHIP

Asking for Major Gifts

The Role of Board and Staff Members

There is only one almost-sure method of soliciting and obtaining major gifts: meeting in person with the potential donor-investor. The knowledge of the agency's work shown by the solicitation team can convert a donor to a donor-investor. This leads to high impact philanthropy and transformational giving.

SHIFTING PARADIGMS

As described in the introduction, the traditional philanthropic paradigm has shifted. The new donor-investors are younger, more impatient. They are active investors who may not respond to the traditional methods of solicitation. Having already investigated the work and potential of the agency, they usually seek out the nonprofit agency that interests them, at which time *they* make the proposal of support that will have an impact on your agency and the community.

For traditional board members and professional staff this type of donor-investor can be very challenging. Most agencies are not prepared when a high impact gift is offered to them without warning. In chapter 4 we outline the documents required for a case statement for a transformational gift; if this is kept up to date, whoever meets with an interested new donor-investor will at least have basic information to rely on during their conversation.

This type of unsolicited offer can happen anywhere, but especially in areas of the United States that have given birth to new high-tech industry. There seems to be at least one of those areas located in almost every state.

The Traditional Paradigm: You Have to Actually Ask for the Gift!

There are many ways to ask for a gift. Throughout this book we have stressed a more sophisticated way to solicit major givers: We want your nonprofit to consider the long term and to convert the major giver to a donor-investor, who then becomes a transformational giver.

The process of asking for a major gift was not invented by the authors, or for that matter by any one brilliant fund raiser or lay leader; but the creative process of the ask has been cultivated and chronicled over the years by the authors and their colleagues. The common thread that weaves its way through the fabric of fund-raising is common sense, along with a derivative of the golden rule: Deal with your prospects and donors exactly as you would like them to deal with you!

WHO MAKES THE FIRST GIFT?

Based on the practical advice solicitors always receive when they undergo solicitor-training seminars, you cannot ask for a gift until you have made your own personal commitment. The first gift is made by the chairperson of the board of directors, who is approached by the executive or development director. Depending on the nature of the nonprofit organization, this gift can either be a leadership gift at the high end of the major gift range (as defined by the nonprofit), or a gift of capacity, for example, from a person who has been given the post of chairperson, not because of prominence, or wealth, but because of his or her knowledge, experience, and management capabilities.

A capacity gift is proportionate: a person who makes a gift at capacity, even if it is smaller than the gift they are requestive from another is a strong solicitor. The asker understands the "stretch" gift and can ask others to do the same.

Whatever the situation, the chairperson's gift is the key, because this person is usually the leader of the organization—a catalyst for soliciting the remaining members of the board. If this person makes a capacity gift instead of a major gift, he or she can still solicit major gifts from the other board members and current major gift donors and prospects. Why? Because the other board members usually know of this person's financial circumstances and understand that the results the nonprofit achieves in the community are due to his or her commitment to the agency.

Simultaneously, the board chair should also ask the executive director to make his or her gift so that the ED can talk to all of the senior staff about their gifts. Yes, professional staff members *must*, not should, make gifts to their agencies. Nonprofit professionals are underpaid compared to their for-profit contemporaries, and their gifts will be smaller than average, but the 100 percent support of the professional staff is part of the giving culture of a nonprofit. It is necessary that this arrangement be outlined and emphasized when the individual person is first employed. At many religious organizations the entire staff, from the executive director to the maintenance supervisor, makes a gift. We would suggest that all nonprofits have this policy of staff giving, even if only of a few dollars; it is not the amount, but the intent. The ED and the development director can then report to the board that the entire staff has made a gift, which will reinforce their solicitation of the board members, active lay leadership, and prospects.

With this premise in place, the lay leader and professional staff team can now arrange to solicit the other donor-investors who are active with the agency. Some of these solicitations may be major (as defined by the nonprofit), and some may fall into a lesser category; but to achieve high impact on the nonprofit and the community, all major donors should be seen in person. Communication is the number-one strategy for a successful solicitation.

Many organizations have strict giving levels, such as $1,000 to $2,499, $2,500 to $4,999, and so on; these categories are used to establish societies named after the founder or some other prominent person who has been or is currently associated with the agency. Performing arts organizations, museums, libraries, hospitals, and universities use this technique to excellent advantage.

If your organization is a social service agency or other community organization, these exclusive categories will not be popular with your constituency. How can this be overcome? The only solution is an organizational strategy, followed by a team effort, and a lot of very hard work! Breaking down your various programs into action modules (including administration) and soliciting impact gifts for these modules is one method that is used to overcome the elitist-giving-levels syndrome. Soliciting a selected group of donors for in-kind gifts (e.g., computers, mobile telephones, printing, etc.) is another way to have a specific giving category without actually setting up a special society. Both of these methods can be publicly acknowledged in the nonprofit's newsletter, on its web site, or in the many other ways outlined in the marketing section of Chapter 10.

SOLICITATION TECHNIQUES FOR DONOR-INVESTORS

The following procedures will help you to organize your thoughts, your efforts, and your agency for the solicitation process.

    I. Informing the solicitation team fully about the agency's mission and vision

   II. Researching the prospect (see chapter 8)
      A. Past support of your agency
      B. Personal information from friends and from business and professional associates
      C. Media exposure (newspapers, professional associations, etc.)

  III. Communicating directly with the prospect
      A. Exchanging values; talking to prospects about their reasons for supporting your agency; letting them describe their values and how these values are put to work in the community by your agency
      B. Discussing prospects' interests, both specific ones and those concerning the work of the nonprofit
      C. Describing the impact that the donor-investors' gifts will have on community
      D. Presenting the nonprofit's development case statement

  IV. Presenting opportunities for the donor-investor to participate in the work of the nonprofit
      A. Networking with colleagues (one of the most important volunteer positions a donor-investor can perform); meeting with peers and telling them about the work the agency does in the community (provides both marketing and stewardship)
      B. Committee assignment based on the donor-investor's interests and background
      C. Letting the donor-investor suggest what he or she would like to work on with the agency

   V. Determining a realistic amount to ask the giver to donate
      A. Reviewing the agency's research
      B. Newtithing™ guidelines
      C. History of past contributions
      D. Personal knowledge of donor-investor's capacity

A MODEL SOLICITATION

The following is a true story, although the names have been changed. We have organized the story using the preceding outline to give you an idea of how the process works.

Informing the Solicitation Team Fully about the Agency's Mission and Vision

The agency is a prominent international organization that aids refugees in every country in which it can operate openly, and in some where it has to use subterfuge. It has been active for more than 75 years and is headquartered in New York City, with regional offices around the United States and in the major European and Asian countries. The agency's main funding comes from its U.S. supporters through the regional offices. Programs are formulated in the New York office and disseminated throughout the satellite offices around the world. Most satellite offices simply rubber-stamp these plans, but in the 1990s, some of these offices and their supporters decided they wanted more say in planning and carrying out the agency's programs. This came about when a number of refugees were to be resettled in the United States and the regional offices were given the task of helping the refugees assimilate into the local community. The overall budget of the agency was not adequate for this huge endeavor and had no time to prepare.

Researching the Prospect

One regional office located on the Pacific coast was given extra people to help, and, to make matters worse, the office was undergoing a change of executive directors at the time. Fortunately, the new director was a young staff person who'd been promoted from another regional office; he had spent all of his professional career with this one agency and knew its programs and problems inside out. Another piece of luck was that the regional development professional was knowledgeable—she knew all of the lay leadership (having lived in the area all of her life) and she possessed creative personal and marketing skills. Although these two individuals had not articulated the strategy of high impact philosophy per se, they knew that the only way they could rebuild after the damage of past donor neglect and at the same time build a working emergency committee was to create a close relationship with the "movers and shakers" of the agency. In order to build this committee they needed a leader, a person with passion, knowledge, and money. Working with the lay leadership, these two professionals had compiled a list of potential board and advisory committee members with the potential to light a fire under this emergency fund-raising drive, and the ability to lead the effort to a successful conclusion and help build a new development structure.

    The agency's new ED was well trained. He immediately began to make appointments to meet with potential emergency committee members, both to get to know them and to find out how difficult this drive was going to be (he did not have the luxurious option of reporting to New York that it could not be accomplished). He was wise enough to insist that a board member or prominent supporter accompany him on these appointments.

Communicating Directly with the Prospect

The first few meetings with the prospects went fairly well and the ED received verbal pledges of support, each of which he immediately confirmed in a thank-you letter, which read like the one found in Exhibit 9.1.

One potential committee member, however, had a completely different agenda. He was not averse to helping the refugees—in fact, he had a lot of experience in this area, although he was a professional in another field. But he was very surprised that the new executive director had telephoned him for an appointment and had brought the board president with him. As the potential committee member pointed out, he had not made a significant gift to the agency since he had been asked to become a member of the board!

Discussing Prospective Donors' Interests and Values

This donor prospect went on to relate what had happened at his first board meeting. As is common in such cases he was asked to say a few words about his background and his interests. He stated his delight at being asked to become a member of the agency's board because he had followed the work of the agency for many years, due to his deep personal interest in the refugee problem. He was not a person to beat around any bush, and he proceeded to relate his ideas on what the agency could accomplish in the refugee world. It seems that these comments ruffled the feathers of a few of the long-time members who had been on the board for many years; but, most of all, he presented a threat to the former executive director, or so the director thought. From that time until the recent telephone call from the new executive director, he had been ignored—politely, but still ignored.

Describing the Impact that the Donor-Investor's Gift Will Have on the Community

Why, asked the new executive director, did you (the donor prospect) remain on the board? The answer was surprising: "I know there are other social service agencies I could support, but their refugee programs are just one of many programs they accomplish in the community. Your agency devotes all of its energy to refugees, in the U.S. and overseas. Our values are the same. Our goals are the same! And, I am a stubborn person and I keep on trying to change the system."

EXHIBIT 9.1 Model Letter

Dear Supporter,

Thank you for meeting with me on such short notice. Your knowledge of our agency and the impending arrival of new refugees made me feel that our work does not go unnoticed.

Your gracious offer of in-kind support, supplying computers and printers, the funds to train our staff in the intricacies of operating the equipment, and the funds (up to an initial grant of $25,000) to teach staff members English is greatly appreciated.

One of our staff will be working with you and your organization, giving you the names and backgrounds of those people who need your help. We are in the process of establishing a temporary center where training can take place, and we will notify you when the center is ready to receive your very generous gift. Thank you for allowing us to use your name in our marketing materials. It will send a very positive message to many potential donors.

On behalf of the board of directors and our entire staff, we are

Sincerely yours,

| [Philanthropist] | Newkid Onblock |
| President | Executive Director |

Letting the Donor-Investor Suggest What He or She Would Like to Do

At this point the ED and the board president knew that they had found the chairman of the emergency committee and a potential donor-investor. Here was a board member who knew the agency's mission statement as well as any staff person; his values were the same; he was just waiting to work with the nonprofit on their programs and to benefit the community.

Personal Knowledge of the Donor-Investor's Capacity

The ED had been briefed by the development director of what to expect as a gift from each person he was going to interview. This person was on the bottom of the list for current and past contributions, but he was near the top of the potential capacity list. It appeared that all he needed was an opportunity to be a donor-investor.

The End Result

The scenario we've described took place 14 years ago. The new board member who had been ignored started to work closely with the new ED; he opened up vistas that no one had ever thought of. He went on-site overseas to direct programs that freed thousands of refugees from starvation and early death, relocating them to friendly countries so they could start their lives over again. In the United States he travelled to other regional offices to talk to his peers about what they could do, based on his experience. He took leadership roles in his home region and helped recruit prominent lay leaders to join the board of directors. He financed all of this out of his own pocket.

When this donor-investor was first approached his yearly gift was $200 to $300 per year; currently he is giving more than $50,000 yearly, and he has started a charitable trust of more than $100,000. He is still an independent, iconoclastic supporter; his gifts arrive addressed to the development director, containing checks of $5 to $10,000. No note or explanation, just the check. This man's involvement was brought about by one person who was willing to listen.

No strategy is implemented in one day, and high impact philanthropy cannot begin to affect your community overnight—but it will in time. Just take the first step. Make that extra effort.

THE CONCEPT OF NEWTITHING™

A few years ago a concerned philanthropist, Claude Rosenberg, Jr., who also happened to be a very successful financial investment advisor, decided to take an in-depth look at philanthropic giving in the United States. The results of this investigation were published in the book *Wealthy and Wise: How You and America Can Get the Most Out of Your Giving.* (New York: Little, Brown & Company, 1994.) What he found evolved into the philosophy of what he now calls newtithing™. *Old* tithing was the time-honored practice of making a gift of 10% of one's current income to philanthropy; originally, in biblical times, that tenth part was given to religious institutions. *Newtithing*™ takes this concept a step forward, considering both your current income and your investment income! Rosenberg defines newtithing™ in these words: "-n., 1. determining comfortably affordable donations to charity based on annual surplus income and the market value, after debt, of investment assets (excluding personal housing)."

What does this mean for the donor-investor?

To make a contribution based only on annual income (which is the norm) is to underinvest in the nonprofit whose values the donor is trying to advance. At the beginning of a new millennium, one that follows many years of increased investment values, contributors (even those with modest annual incomes and investments), no matter what their tax brackets, are denying themselves the joy of furthering the nonprofit's vision and values. The donor can perform this act of philanthropy without changing his or her lifestyle. The extra income derives from returns on the donor-investor's stocks, corporate or municipal bonds, investment real estate, business partnerships, and so on. As defined previously, the assets used to calculate a donor-investor's charitable contribution should not include his or her personal residence and should account for normal living expenses.

It is easy to be a financial whiz with other people's money, telling them what they should do with their hard-earned income. Each of us has preconceived ideas about how we want to use our surplus earnings. The purpose of this book is not to be an investment advisor to potential major givers. What we do hope to do is open up new vistas for the donor-investor, guiding him or her along a path that leads to satisfied giving. Newtithing™ is one of those vistas.

Let's set up a fictional scenario and make a few assumptions based on some facts and figures. Tom and Mary Morgan are both well educated, intelligent senior managers in the high technology business; they are also young (mid-thirties) and have just purchased their first home. They saved for the down payment after first paying off their college loans. Their respective companies have done very well and have done well by them. After making the down payment on their home, their stock options suddenly became very valuable and their salaries increased to the point that they have no immediate financial worries. They are what we call "high-tech boomers."

Their combined gross salaries amount to $250,000; their savings and investment portfolio amounts to $900,000. Their charitable contributions, however, only amount to $5,000. The investment portfolio yields a surplus of $50,000, but only $20,000 of this is hands-on cash. The remainder is the increased value of their corporate stock options, which cannot be realized until they are converted to actual shares of stock.

Implementing the Concept of Newtithing™

You may wonder how to put such great theory into practice. The most effective way to explore Newtithing™ is through NewTitheCalc, the first web-based philanthropic planner that helps determine a comfortably affordable charitable giving level each year based on an individuals personal finances. NewTitheCalc is at: http://www.newtithing.org and can be posted on a non-profit web site to dovetail with one-on-one education or advisory services, group seminars, on-line giving facilities, and major donor programs. NewTitheCalc may also help you determine how much to ask a donor-investor before you meet with them.

Complemented by a suite of educational information on philanthropy and giving patterns, NewTitheCalc allows users to enter an array of financial data to explore affordable giving levels. Users can theorize on how a change in any aspect of their finances would affect their giving wherewithal, and how a particular giving level would affect their net worth. Further, the laws and definitions that comprise the calculator's help buttons offer a virtual seminar in the tax and financial aspects of philanthropic planning.

Further, the senior professional staff members in many nonprofit organizations are close to one or more of the current major givers. This closeness might allow them to talk candidly with those individuals about their giving and to ask them to become the first donor-investors for the agency, and to lead the way for newtithing™ by heading up a committee to educate other major givers and potential donor-investors (many of whom are probably already sitting on your board and/or executive committee).

CONCLUSION

If your nonprofit is small in regard to total funds raised but not on community impact, and if your largest major gift is in the $250 to $750 range, don't give up hope. You've taken the first step—you're reading the book you need.

The I.R.S. has just released its latest figures on income in the United States. The figures are for the 1998 tax year, but they indicate a trend that is growing very briskly. Comparing 1998 to 1997, the I.R.S. shows that the number of returns in the $50,000 to $100,000 range increased from 21.7 to 23.1 million. In the $100,000-plus category, the number of returns increased from 7.2 to 8.3 million. There were 2.5 million more potential donor-investors by the end of 1998 than there were in 1997—but a total of 31.4 million potential donor-investors remain to work with, to meet, and to start the stewardship process.

Your agency might consider itself tiny, but it has the opportunity to use the information in this chapter to increase its donor-investor base and, consequently, its total revenue.

We have given you many tools to use, but let us repeat the two most important:

1. Always meet current and potential donor-investors in person.
2. Communicate—Communicate—Communicate!

10 Getting Your Share

How to Market Your Issues

to the Community

In a survey conducted early in 2000 for *Shine!,* an online philanthropy channel, the research firm Roper Starch Worldwide found that "nearly 70 million Americans who want to be charitable don't donate their time or money to charities because they know too little about those organizations." In the high-growth market of nonprofits, getting your message out is increasingly important. However, name recognition is not enough. Much more is at stake when nonprofits set out to make themselves known to their communities. Because we are values-based, and because we depend on people's investment of time and money for our success, we need to make sure that our *marketing* is values-based. It is not enough to tell people about our organizations and what we do; First, we have to connect them with the reasons we exist (the issue) and the values our work advances.

Along with this information, we need to let our constituencies know how effective their investment in us is—what we do with their investment, and the difference our work, supported by their investment, makes in the community. This is essential. Eighty-four percent of respondents, according to the report appearing on Shine! reportedly had little faith in the nonprofit sector's ability to put the money to good use, and another 76 percent said they were hesitant to give because they did not know enough about the organization's goals. This response can only be an outgrowth of the kind of marketing and fund-raising that nonprofits have practiced for too long—sending messages that are based on the needs they have, not on the needs they meet (Grace, 1997). The best way to communicate a nonprofit's goals is by describing the impact of their successes: more children adopted, more seniors living their lives with dignity and care, more people enjoying and learning from the music provided by the community orchestra, or more women in South Asian villages able to begin their own businesses. The goals are implicit in these reports and move the investment motivation from speculation to affirmation of values.

The Roper report concludes with two other powerful findings. According to the survey, more than half of respondents (58 percent) said they had difficulty finding charitable groups that address causes that are important to them, and 50 percent reported having trouble locating charities in their communities (GB3 Group marketing e-mail newsletter).[1]

The first of the concluding findings reinforces the premise of much of this book: People's giving, particularly of transformational gifts, is focused on issues. They want to find the organizations that address the issues they feel are most important to the community and to themselves. Our marketing, which is so often institution-focused rather than solution-focused, tells them about an organization whose merit, relative to their interests, may not be apparent. This is particularly true when the name of the organization may not be directly or immediately linked to its issue or service. But we persist in focusing first on our organization, and then on telling people about the issues we address. We must reverse that order if we are to attract transformational and other gifts to our organizations.

The second of those final findings—the difficulty the respondents had in finding organizations in their communities in which to invest— is also a function of marketing. We need to position the organizations in our communities as the vehicles through which people can help solve community problems and provide community enhancements; but we also need to let them know that we exist, that we are effective, and that as a sector we are a good investment. Going beyond the marketing of individual organizations, we need to network with other nonprofits in our communities to educate people about the impact of what we do. We need to raise the level of understanding about the role of the nonprofit sector and why it is the vigorous alternative to government funding and the flexible alternative to purely private support. Because we do institution-focused marketing (when we do marketing at all) and because we sense an implicit competition with other nonprofits, we tend to do little if any broad marketing of the importance of investing in nonprofits. In so doing, we end up diminishing our own po-

1 "Strengthening the Nonprofit Marketing & Communications Infrastructure," briefing for White House Conference on Philanthropy, May 23, 2000.

tential resources. People have difficulty understanding our sector—particularly in countries outside of the United States where philanthropy is just maturing—and part of our marketing mandate must be to build confidence in nonprofit investment overall, not just in our organizations.

The Roper report, as summarized by *Shine!* tells us first and foremost that the nonprofit sector needs to market itself more effectively. In its marketing, our sector needs to set out the benefits of investing, both in terms of return on values (Grace, 1997) and benefits to our clients and the community. Too often, nonprofits shy away from marketing because they fear it will look like "advertising," or because they think it is too bold, too expensive, or not a priority. For organizations with important missions that are seeking transformational investments, this is a time for boldness. The cost of marketing need not be prohibitive, and there is no greater priority.

WHAT NONPROFITS CAN LEARN FROM FOR-PROFITS ABOUT MARKETING

For-profit corporations and companies know how to position their marketing to strike at the customer's values. They spend hundreds of thousands of dollars studying the beliefs and motivations of potential customers and then cast their messages using those values to promote their product. People either succumb to the message and buy the product or service, or they feel resentful about the blatant manipulation of their values and are turned off. Fortunately, we know very few well-managed nonprofits that use blatantly manipulative marketing approaches used by many for-profit companies, but we can learn from the for-profit marketing and advertising strategies that confront us daily.

PRODUCT VERSUS BENEFIT: BASIC MARKETING STRATEGY

Advertising today for products and services is much less about the product or service than it is about the benefit of that product or service to the consumer. Appeals to consumers have become much more focused on marketing, and much less like standard advertising. In marketing, an exchange principle exists: Based on their knowledge of a particular market segment's interests and habits, companies or corporations promote the long-term benefits an individual will receive in exchange for their purchase of a particular product or service. With advertising, in which knowledge of the needs and interests of the market may be more limited, the appeal is based much less on the long-term benefit than on the point-of-purchase immediate gain of buying the product or service. The new marketing approach goes beyond advertising's emphasis on acquisitions. Likewise, our nonprofits must learn to focus their outreach on marketing their issues and values, not just on acquiring donors. They must internalize and practice the exchange process. The exchange principle, in which the benefits of making an investment are emphasized, is the fulcrum of the nonprofit's transaction with a donor. We need to insert this same marketing principle into our community outreach and into the very context of our transformational giving programs.

TWO FOR-PROFIT ADVERTISING EXAMPLES

In the for-profit sector, contemporary advertisements have stepped deeply into the marketing arena. Highly market-focused, these advertisements appeal to people's values, and the very best of them connect so well with people's feelings and beliefs that they both try to stimulate purchase and inspire belief in the long-term benefits of the product or service. It is increasingly common to read or view an advertisement and not know until the end what product or service is being offered.

Fireman's Fund, as part of a print advertising series launched in 1999, ran two advertisements whose entire text did not mention Fireman's Fund until the identifying line at the end. The first read: "Life is like a tornado watch. You can hide in the basement until it is over. Or you can stand on the roof, get rockstar hair and shout: 'I knew you were coming, that's why I didn't rake the leaves.'"

The second, appearing shortly thereafter, and characterized with the same kind of semi-abstract artist's illustration, read: "Life is a rush into the unknown. You can duck down and hope nothing hits you, or stand up tall as you can, show your teeth and say, 'Dish it up, baby, and don't be stingy with the jalapeños.'" We have included a third, as well (Exhibit 10.1). The relationship of these very feisty and somewhat inspiring statements to insurance is a stretch, but Fireman's Fund may have felt that the arresting nature of both advertisements would connect with people's values and get their attention more readily than more traditional advertisements. (See Exhibit 10.1.)

Ford Motor Company, in late 1999 and early 2000, did a series of insert advertisements in high-end consumer magazines in the United States. A 10-page, four-color, glossy foldout, its cost would clearly be out of reach and inappropriate for most nonprofits. However, its potential impact is not out of reach because it uses (some would say "exploits") people's values to promote the benefits of their product. The opening page of the insert has three photographs, none of which display cars: mountains at the top, a blurred clock in the middle, and a rocky wilderness area at the bottom. The text, printed over the clock face, reads, "We build walls. With our everyday routines. And our cram-it-all-in schedules. Walls that make a nasty habit of separating us from our dreams." No mention of cars, or Ford. Opening the insert, the reader sees the black-and-white image of a Ford Excursion (a sport utility vehicle), the specifications of which are written in approximately 8-point type, set perpendicular to the image—a text that runs the entire length of the foldout ad, barely readable by unassisted eyes. Opposite that image, however, is a starfish in green on a green background. Over the starfish is written, "But, what if there *were* no walls?" The next page folds out with a black and white image of a Ford Expedition, and opposite it is a dried, muddy footprint of a bear, done in shades of yellow across which is written, "What if there were a way to break straight through to your dreams?" Another foldout—a black and white image of a Ford Explorer—follows, and opposite it, in rich burnt sienna, is the image of a fossilized shell, across which is printed, "There is. All you need is an outfitter with the right equipment. Ford is your outfitter. Outfitting you with the most far-reaching sport utility vehicles on earth." The message is not done: two more foldouts follow, both of SUVs in black and white, and over the final one is the Ford Outfitters' logo, which says, "No Boundaries/Ford Outfitters," below which is written, "Climb in. And watch the walls come tumbling down."

Many people were put off by this ad—because of the money spent, the seeming manipulation of values, or because SUVs are not fuel-efficient in a fuel-scarce world. Whatever the reaction, however, it is important to pay attention to the way in which the ad captures what they would have you perceive as a benefit. They base their marketing on the solution they say they offer: They will ease the time pressures in our lives by outfitting us with a recreational vehicle that will restore our sense of leisure and help reconnect us with the things that matter. They draw our attention by focusing on the realities of our overburdened pace of living. By juxtaposing the symbols of the natural environment with their automobiles, they lend

EXHIBIT 10.1 Fireman's Fund: Successful Marketing in the For-Profit Sector

business & personal insurance

Fireman's Fund®

License to get on with it.™

A company of the Allianz Group

EXHIBIT 10.1 (Continued)

THE UNKNOWN

YOU CAN DUCK DOWN AND HOPE NOTHING HITS YOU,

OR STAND UP TALL AS YOU CAN, SHOW IT YOUR TEETH

AND SAY

DISH IT UP, BABY,
AND DON'T BE STINGY WITH THE JALAPEÑOS.

EXHIBIT 10.1 Fireman's Fund: Successful Marketing in the For-Profit Sector (Continued)

EXHIBIT 10.1 (Continued)

NG A KITE

YOU CAN KEEP IT ON A SHORT LEASH,

OR LET OUT BIG GULPS OF STRING UNTIL YOU BREAK THE CLOUD COVER

AND THINK

IF THAT GETS ANY HIGHER,
IT'LL NEED BEVERAGE SERVICE.

Used with permission of The Fireman's Fund.

sway to the notion that these cars can reconnect us with a less pressured life.

WHY NONPROFIT MARKETING STRATEGIES MUST CHANGE

What we learn from this advertisement is the power of marketing benefits or solutions, not just the product. In our nonprofit mission statements we focus too much on our organizations, and not enough on the reason we provide our services (the need we are meeting). Further, when we state our accomplishments, we are much more likely to stress how much money we have raised than to translate that achievement into benefits for the community. We must convey to our communities *why* we exist (see the Roper study feedback that opened this chapter) so they can understand the importance of what we do and know that we are worthy of their investment.

This has never been more important. With the swing among transformational donor-investors to focus on issues, rather than institutions, we must identify and market the issues we address and the benefits of investing. Apple Computer, in its early days, gained part of IBM's market share with a simple and powerful approach: it marketed *solutions* while IBM continued to market *hardware*.

SUCCESSFUL MARKETING APPLICATIONS FROM THE NONPROFIT SECTOR

Two separate marketing efforts, occurring more than a decade apart and costing very little relative to their impact, reflect a strong use of values that do not manipulate or offend. They instruct us about effective marketing.

New York City Opera

More than a decade ago, a touring opera company in New Jersey was promoting a production of *Aida* that would include, among other things, live elephants. The staging drew criticism for its lavish production at the cost of artistic merit, and its critics were particularly skeptical of the elephants that were to appear. Coincidentally, the New York City Opera had recently used the slogan "No Elephants" on the cover of a subscription brochure (see Exhibit 10.2). The timing, though inadvertent, could not have been better. The message was a values-based presentation of why the New York City Opera was important to the community. The cover was solid turquoise, with white lettering that simply said, "No Elephants." Inside, the text continued, "No plodding plots, no ponderous parades, nothing stuffy. Nothing musty. No masquerades or Moorish ballets. Just the things that really matter—the music and drama, and above all, the human voice raised to the limits of its expressive power." It continued with an invitation to "Join [then general director] Christopher Keene and New York City Opera as they transport you across the centuries. As they lead you into a world of extraordinary works by Mozart, Donizetti, Sondheim, and more . . ."

This inexpensive brochure was part of a clever series produced in 1990 that also included a brochure entitled "Daring Do," in a clever play on words (Exhibit 10.2). Each offered opportunities for investment. Those materials were highly successful, very witty and intelligent, and reflective of the values embraced by the New York City Opera: a highly creative and accessible alternative to the more traditional Metropolitan Opera.

Sage Hill School

A very different tone and approach, but with the same focus on benefits, has been taken by Sage Hill School (whose values-motivated transformational gifts are described in Chapter 5).

Its values, as described previously, have guided every publication and decision beginning with the planning stages. As a result, the community clearly understands why the school, which opened in September 2000, was formed, and has expectations of the kinds of students it will produce and the way in which they will be taught. The school, in its marketing materials to students and the community, has been transparent about its beliefs and benefits. In their brochure sent in response to inquiries about the school from prospective students and parents, they carried through with the values-orientation that had characterized all of their outreach, as seen in Exhibit 10.3. Following the theme of their viewbook—"The tradition begins with you"—this smaller brochure successfully captured and conveyed the mission and values. The cover reads: "Sage Hill School . . . The tradition begins with you. Teach students to love knowledge and they will learn for the rest of their lives. Inspire students to use knowledge productively, with courage and compassion, and they will change the world." Inside, the left panel is dominated by the word "commitment," running vertically next to three blocks of text: "A commitment to excellence," "A commitment to diversity,"

EXHIBIT 10.2 New York City Opera: Successful Marketing in the Nonprofit Sector

N E W   Y O R K   C I T Y   O P E R A   1 9 9 0   S E A S O N

Daring Do.

N O W   T H R O U G H   N O V E M B E R   1 8

EXHIBIT 10.2 (Continued)

Used with permission of the New York City Opera.

Sage Hill School

THE **TRADITION** BEGINS WITH YOU

Teach students
     to love knowledge and they will learn
  for the rest of their lives.

Inspire students
    to use knowledge productively,
  with courage and compassion,
      and they will change the world.

EXHIBIT 10.3   invitational postcard (Continued)

Used with the permission of the Sage School.

and "A commitment to community." Well-written, with plenty of action verbs and well-drawn adjectives, this page is opposite a three-color center-fold panel that states, "Welcome to Sage Hill, where students, parents, and teachers are creating a new kind of high school. Rigorous and rewarding, committed to diversity, deeply connected to our community—Sage Hill is where remarkable students are growing into the leaders of tomorrow." Four words float on this panel, reflecting the text opposite: excellence, community, integrity, and balance. Inside, on the panel behind the three-color panel, the mission words continue from the front cover: "Challenge students to achieve and they will excel. Encourage teamwork and you will teach leadership. Broaden students' horizons and they will find new frontiers." That panel and the next two focus on faculty and curriculum, including a boxed section of text about the faculty—"Faculty: Setting standards, setting examples"—which states, "The best teachers do not just teach—they participate fully in the life of their school. They communicate, share, guide, coach and inspire. They question, counsel, support, and challenge. Most important, they model the attitudes and behaviors that transform students into informed, engaged citizens." The last panel is a tear-off inviting further inquiry, which finishes by reminding readers that Sage Hill is "A diverse, talented, thoughtful school community" where "As we pioneer together, we will do more than break new ground. We will make new traditions—and they may very well begin with you."

With all Sage Hill materials, the colors (sage-green and gray), logo (a sage leaf), type face, texture, and tone are consistent. Lined up side-by-side, they are thematically connected and visually pleasing. They have successfully branded the school; people now recognize Sage Hill materials when they receive them. An invitation to one of several open houses used Sage Hill green, the sage leaf logo, and the mission: "Sage Hill School will instill in its students a love of knowledge and the ability to use that knowledge productively, courageously, and compassionately throughout their lives." On the large postcard (Exhibit 10.3), recipients were invited to "Discover Sage Hill School. The tradition begins with you. Opening Fall 2000." Paper quality is sturdy, but not overly textured and not glossy. The materials look substantial, but not expensive.

The power of consistency is mighty. In the considerable coverage the school has received in the local and regional press, the media has respected and explored the school's values. This has provided even more opportunity to convey what the benefits of a Sage Hill education will be to the community in general, and particularly to those who will be interested in and capable of making transformational investments.

Effective marketing is not about gloss or expense; it is about a compelling message delivered in ways that are appropriate to the organization and the audience. Those venues for promotion are increasing with the new media, and web site and e-mail marketing offer new opportunities, as well as new challenges, to nonprofit organizations.

Branding, which became a marketing buzz word at the end of the twentieth century, is not a gimmick. Developing materials and themes that are repeated in all of your outreach is one way to establish wider recognition in the community. One children's service organization reviewed its materials and realized that nothing matched. A venerable organization, providing excellent services for more than 40 years, they were not well known except among volunteers, clients, and referring professionals. A larger, more visible organization was frequently perceived as incorporating this particular nonprofit, and contributions (including bequests) often came to the smaller organization with the other organization's name. The confusion people felt about the organization was derived from two realities: the proximity of the more visible organization with a similar name, and the absence of any consistency in marketing the smaller organization. Realizing that a capital campaign planned for some years hence would require higher community recognition, the board and staff implemented a low-budget but highly effective plan. Over the course of two years, marketing and fund-raising materials developed an image that effectively conveyed just who they were, what they did, and how effective they had been. Using black-and-white photography only, they developed an image that was unmistakable. Two years into the program, people would include notes with their contributions saying how much they looked forward to receiving the materials with "photographs of those beautiful children."

MARKETING: A MATTER OF TIME

Our tendency is to shift marketing approaches too quickly when one doesn't seem to be working. We do not allow sufficient time for building an image or conveying a message. We are impatient for results and forget that in our message-laden environment it takes longer to get people's attention. Market research done in the 1990s revealed that it can take up to seven "hits" before people begin to absorb the image and message and respond to it. When evaluating our marketing and fund-raising programs, we need to remember this. Most organizations do not spend sufficient time figuring out just what it is they want to convey in their materials and outreach, which is why they fall back to talking about themselves, instead of about their impact or the issues.

To be effective with marketing, organizations need to do the following:

1. Develop a theme based on values, impacts, and issues. If marketing and image development are high priorities for your organization, recruit talented and willing advisors to your board or to a special marketing committee. Engage them around the task and be prepared to listen to their advice and act on it.
2. Develop a sequence of materials and images for print, web sites, and public service announcements and other media use that will extend over a period of years with annual fine tuning of the presentation, but not the basic theme. If your organization is very low-budget, with minimum resources, shop for opportunities to receive pro bono help with these efforts. There are advertising and marketing firms in every community that have a commitment to provide pro bono services to one or more nonprofits.
3. Devote a portion of your budget to creating and regularly revising these materials. Some budget support is essential, even if you receive generous pro bono help. By putting marketing into your budget, you sensitize the board and staff to its importance and ensure that it will be a financial priority.

4. Evaluate your impact, but don't rush to judgment. Experiment with different approaches to the same message. If your goal is to build transformational giving, then convey the ways in which your organization is transforming your community and how those involved have been or will be transformed by their involvement. The annual fund for one independent school used this approach over a period of several years, producing materials that resembled each other, each conveying a different story about the impact of investment on the students, faculty, and community. Very powerful, it was both award-winning and effective in raising the size of annual gifts. Your first efforts may not seem to generate the desired results, but resist the temptation to change the message. Wait until it sinks in.

With these basic guideposts, even the smallest organization can undertake a values-based marketing program that will focus on issues and impact. There are other principles as well.

HOW TO MARKET YOUR ORGANIZATION

Selecting the right way in which to market your organization is critical. Before selecting a vehicle, it is important to know how to market with impact so you can attract donors at all levels, including those who can transform your organization.

MARKETING WITH IMPACT

Using the acronym IMPACT (Impression, Message, Product, Ability, Case, and Timing), we can evaluate each of the aspects of effective values-driven marketing.

Impression

What impression are you trying to convey? What impression are you currently making with your materials, your public relations, and your formal and informal advocacy? Nearly all of the transforming gifts raised by the San Francisco Food Bank in its campaign during the 1990s were motivated by the impression the Food Bank conveyed of an organization that put its money into programs, not into public relations, fund-raising, marketing, or administration. Key investors perceived an organization that was capable of fulfilling its mission and one that was appropriately, not excessively, staffed. The early support of a major corporation, long involved in food drives with its employees, was based on this perception, and that attracted others. One of the largest individual donors initially winced over the idea of participating in a project that was raising $5 million for what is, essentially, a warehouse. However, the administrative and campaign leaders were able to support every dollar of the goal by linking it to the program, and to explain why investments needed to be made to include freezers, sorting rooms, and other aspects of the building. The campaign materials, developed midway through the funding program, were done pro bono by a highly esteemed advertising agency. They, too, were consistent with the image that the food bank was conveying. Simple, two-color, and to the point: "People are hungry. There's plenty of food. So, what's the problem?" The problem was the lack of an adequate facility for processing food and getting it out to more than 300 agencies. The materials were based on the findings from a widely reported study on hunger in the San Francisco Bay Area. They were an invitation to invest in one solution to the problem of hunger.

Message

Use bold words and images. Too much of the material coming out of the nonprofit sector is tedious, overwritten, and passive. Talk about the need you are meeting, not the need you have. Focus on the children, the seniors, the athletes, and the disabled you serve. Tell their stories, and inform people of the impact your organization is having on the larger community by successfully serving the needs of your clients. Because we are organizations with a serious purpose, we tend to sacrifice spontaneous and interesting messages for those that are dull. You can honor your serious purpose better by employing language that engages readers who open your mail, visit your web site, or meet with you. You are competing for potential investor's attention along with other direct marketing organizations. People increasingly shop for their charitable investments much the way they shop for other ways to invest their discretionary funds. Promote the issues you are helping to meet and the impact you are having, and let people know the benefits of investing. The message need not be delivered in an expensive vehicle—the power lies in the message you convey.

Product

What is your product? Why would someone want to make a transforming investment? Once you identify and convey the issues you work with and the values that drive your programs, you need to describe your product. Use everyday language. Spare the jargon. Too much of the material that comes from our sector describes a product that the uninformed investor cannot easily understand. Keep the descriptions simple, accurate, and inviting. Update your materials, particularly your web site, frequently. Few things are more off-putting than out-of-date information.

Ability

What makes your organization the best investment for people interested in this particular issue? What is your track record relative to your stated mission? Why do people invest in your organization, rather than (or together with) another similar organization? Accomplishments need not be presented in a boastful way. Information about your ability and impact can be given through the eyes and words of others. Your ability is also keyed to your financial information. People need to see that you are cost-effective and can ably deliver your programs. It is one of the ways they measure ability.

Case

The oldest principle in fund-raising is still the strongest. Transformational gifts, and all other gifts, come from people who understand your case and believe in it. What is your case for support? Can you articulate it—and do you—clearly, succinctly, and powerfully? Is the case pegged to the needs you meet, rather than the needs you have? Does your full array of case materials include goals, objectives, and back-up information about the programs and people supported and other information that a potential transformational donor might request? The case, including mission, should be reviewed annually during the planning process. Keep it fresh, vital, and available.

Timing

Timing in nonprofit marketing is about consistency and opportunity. Because we don't always know the internal timing that governs a person's decision to make a transforming investment, or any investment, in an organization, we have to be consistent with our outreach and messages. We need to keep the information pipeline full of issues and impact-related morsels that can be accessed by a prospective donor-investor. Increasingly, donors are setting their own giving schedules. Moved by an issue, or by their own personal circumstances, they may slow down or accelerate a process over which we used to feel we had control. Our job is to develop and regularly communicate the messages that will inspire a donor to think of our organization when reviewing the array of institutions that are dealing with an issue of importance to them. Consistency is a virtue in this case, and so is the ability to respond quickly and appropriately to opportunities that arise. As a sector, we are too process-driven, which often irritates potential donors. Our market timing must be governed by a commitment to responsiveness outside of an established process, and a willingness to collapse several well-learned steps in the donor development process if the donor's timing is on a faster schedule than ours. If an existing large donor refers one of her friends to you as a potential transforming donor, don't feel you have to go through the usual steps. The door has been opened. Call that person or e-mail them the information that your existing investor feels is important. To delay can create two levels of loss: loss of confidence from the existing donor, and loss of an important gift from the potential donor.

CONCLUSION

Market your values and impact, along with the issues you are working with. Embed the marketing of your organization, as well as its needs, within the larger and more attractive marketing of the way your organization meets the needs of your clients and investors by linking to the values and visions that truly inspire them.

Transforming gifts are values-based. Make sure your marketing is, too.

Maintaining Your Major Donors

Critical Stewardship Practices

Stewardship is probably the most neglected aspect of donor and fund development. Confusing recognition with stewardship, organizations will proudly point to the recognition levels within their major donor programs as the way they keep in touch with their donors. Recognition is important, but it is not enough.

If we view stewardship as a philosophical commitment to and respect for both the source and impact of a gift (Grace, 1997) then we realize that it goes beyond donor recognition. Stewardship is a process that begins with a person's first gift and proceeds on an unbroken continuum throughout the span of that funder's relationship with the organization. Some key points about stewardship at all levels of philanthropy are important:

1. *The best stewardship is based not on what the organization wants to do for the donor, but on what the donor would like in terms of recognition and involvement.* In some cases, the best stewardship may be to respect the donor's wish to be left alone.
2. *Although most stewardship programs are directed appropriately toward major and transformational donors, all donors should be recognized and communicated with, no matter the size of their gift.* The profile of donors is changing. They are not as easily recognizable, they are less traditional, and they are often younger, from diverse cultures, and new to giving. By arbitrarily setting internal benchmarks for initial recognition (i.e., only donors of

$500 or more receive a personal thank you note), we neglect the obvious: A donor of $100 may have the current capacity or eventual inclination to give much more. To ignore the first gift may make it the last.

3. *Nonprofit stewardship is an educational process for new donors.* Younger donors, and others new to philanthropy, learn about the philanthropic process from the ways in which they are treated by nonprofits. The response made by organizations to their gifts can shape the lifetime philanthropic patterns of young donors and can solidify important perceptions about the nonprofit sector in general among seasoned donors as well as those new to philanthropy. Nonprofit organizations need to understand the profound educational role they can play, and realize what neglect of stewardship conveys about the sector as a whole. It is a tremendous responsibility.

4. *The IRS, in the United States, and common sense, throughout the world, tell us that, with few exceptions, providing costly "give-backs" to donors for their gifts is not a sound practice.* Increasingly, donors look to organizations to spend all of the money on the purpose for which it is intended, rather than on plaques or other forms of recognition. If some of the more traditional donors still need these forms of recognition, provide them. Others are much more satisfied with those mementos that remind them of the mission: a thank you letter from the scholarship recipient, a drawing from the homeless child in the community art program, a photograph of the production the donor sponsored. Scale the recognition to a level appropriate to the organization's image and budget. Stewardship is yet another form of marketing and needs to be consistent with the impact you are trying to create and focused on the donor's needs and interests.

5. *Promote the nontangible benefits as the core of your stewardship.* Connect your donors constantly to your products and services. Invite them to open rehearsals and lectures. Give them hard hat tours of building(s) under construction or program tours of established agencies or schools. Find ways to involve them around the issues and impact you have created.

6. *Position stewardship as part of the transformation, rather than the transaction.* Making the distinction in the stewardship process between transaction and transformation is a strong way to make the distinction between the philosophical bases of these two processes for donors. If stewardship is perceived by the donor as transactional—send a plaque, write a letter, put the name on the wall to close the "deal"—then the kind of relationship that leads to truly transformational giving may be jeopardized. Personalize the stewardship for maximum impact. Write handwritten notes. Make the occasional phone call just to update an investor about something wonderful that has happened. At board meetings, when sur-

rounded by many transformational investors, be sure to observe the "SOS" part of the agenda: "share our success." Tell a story that conveys the way in which their investment is making a difference. Keep the transformational stories fresh and current, and let your donors know of their role in the story you are telling. That information, combined with thoughtful consistent ways to communicate it, will help transform them.

7. *Initiate the stewardship process during the solicitation of the gift.* In the process of negotiating the gift, introduce the options for stewardship. Ask the donor several questions: How would you like to be recognized? What about mailings—where and how do you like to receive them? We would like to involve you in some of our opportunities to get to know our program staff better—is this something you would have time for? By engaging the donor's thinking at the time the gift is made, the transforming process gets underway, and they understand that these are not just transactions. They see that their gifts are valued as investments, and that they are respected as investors.

CONNECTING DONORS WITH PROGRAM

One of the biggest problems with connecting donors and key volunteers with nonprofits is our tendency to move them away from program and closer to administration and fund-raising as they become bigger donors or board members or become more involved as volunteers on committees or advisory boards.

Part of stewardship has to be the continual reconnection of donors and volunteers with program. People are drawn to organizations because of mission, issues, and impact. We reward their increased involvement by connecting them less and less with program and more and more with administrative and volunteer leaders and decision makers. While this is important, particularly for those donors and volunteers who will become leaders, part of effective stewardship has to be constant revitalization through involvement with program. When you link donors and key volunteers with program people, you remind them constantly of the impact of their involvement.

One of the challenges in implementing this program connection involves the concern that some nonprofit CEOs have about donors and volunteers working directly with staff. Some CEOs create communication traps and barriers that cut off access to other staff people except through their offices. While some CEOs say they are protecting their staffs' time, more often it is a lack of self-confidence and trust that undergirds this kind of action. This is a worrisome aspect of nonprofit administration that usually implies poor communication between board and staff leadership. This creates a problem in implementing effective stewardship. It is the responsibility of boards and staff leadership to develop strategies and policies so program staff and volunteers can interact around the mission without the CEO feeling threatened. Ironically, the "looping" function of transformational giving (see Chapter 1) requires this kind of interaction, but it can make less-confident CEOs feel "out of the loop." Organizations committed to improving their stewardship will need to develop communication strategies to avoid this pitfall.

Stewardship that Focuses on Issues, Not Just the Organization

Part of this new kind of stewardship is the importance of committing to focus on issues and impact, not just on the institution. While building "brand loyalty" to your organization has to be a driving force in all stewardship in order to ensure repeated gifts, the transformational giving process requires linking your organization's accomplishments to the larger issues that drive today's philanthropy.

You build loyalty to your organization by focusing on the ways in which you effectively manage gifts to deliver the highest possible program return on the investment, but you provide the true return on values when the donor sees how her investment is affecting larger community or global issues. Donor-investors want to know they are participants in larger solutions that are improving conditions for all preschool teachers and therefore the education of preschool children, making the arts accessible in a community where arts funding from public sources has been cut off, or in raising the standard of living in all developing Southern Hemisphere countries by having an impact on one or more communities.

SYSTEMS AND STEWARDSHIP

Although stewardship is largely a personally interactive process, and is guided greatly by common sense, good listening, and intuition, systems that support the ongoing health of a stewardship program are critical. Be sure you have at least the following to support your stewardship program, particularly if you are positioning yourself for transformational giving:

1. Prepare a program calendar that is kept up to date and is communicated regularly to donors and key volunteers in the ways they like to be communicated with, whether by e-mail, letter, telephone call, or fax.
2. Maintain a tracking system—there is one imbedded in most donor-based management software packages—that computes the number of visits and interactions a person has with your organization, not just in the cultivation process, but in the stewardship process as well.
3. Devise interest-area grids that track your donors according to their interests within your organization and the larger issues that drive those interests. When organized in this way, it is easy to pull up a list of those to invite to a special lecture or presentation.
4. Plan a regular schedule for interacting with your key donors and volunteers, according to how often and in what way they want to interact with you. This should be on the calendar of every development and executive director. This interaction can take place by phone, e-mail, personal visit, or whatever combination of those is appropriate. You will be in a difficult position if you allow too much time between communications and then suddenly need a person's support for a new project or program.
5. Let your key donors and volunteers know when there is bad news as well as good news. With either kind of news, don't let them hear it from someone else first. Use e-mail for good news: Stanford University, in announcing the appointment of John Hennessey as president in April 2000, e-mailed key donors and volunteers with the news on the morning of the day the press conference was to be held. These investors appreciated having inside information before reading it in the newspaper. They felt special. With bad news, a telephone call may be more appropriate, but e-mail may be faster. With any bad news (e.g., a scandal, loss, firing, resignation, client lawsuit), it is important for the organization to take a position so that donors and volunteers know how to discuss it with others in the community. Investor loyalty is eroded by surprises for which they have no information or answers.
6. Support retaining donors in a stewardship program even when their giving lags or stops. If we limit our stewardship to those transformational donors who are "current" in our materials, then we are indicating a shift back to viewing their support as a gift transaction not a transformational investment. An investment has long-term benefit and investors should be afforded recognition and involvement opportunities for as long as the gift has an impact. A truly transformational gift will

have a very long-lasting impact, and the donor should stay involved through your stewardship programs.

7. Post good news on your web site and, with donor permission, let those who visit your site know what a difference an investment can make. Often, these are the stories that can convert a shopper into a buyer. As the profile of donors changes, we know that some will make an initial investment through the internet and then wait for a personal relationship to develop. Don't let them wait too long. Get them into a mutually agreeable stewardship program as soon as that first gift is received.

8. Be sure that the donor's stewardship preferences are documented in their file. Personnel and volunteers may change, but a donor's transforming involvement should not be affected by those changes. Nothing is more damaging to a donor's faith in an organization than to have his or her relationship affected by changes in personnel. It erodes their confidence and can lead them to shift their loyalty to another organization dealing with the same issues.

GETTING LEADERS TO UNDERSTAND THE VALUE OF STEWARDSHIP

As a step in the process of donor development and transformational giving, the value of stewardship cannot be overstated. Even so, it is a function often not budgeted in smaller organizations. Justification for spending money on donor recognition events, or even for subsidizing certain performances or other opportunities to allow donors to bring guests, becomes a battleground for development officers and financial managers. The case must be made for stewardship and cultivation, the two soft sides of solicitation. Although it is easy to track the impact of a direct solicitation by counting the money that comes in, it is difficult to measure the long-term potential impact of an event or program geared toward cultivation (development of the relationship that can lead to a transforming gift) or stewardship (nurturing of the relationship that led to a transforming gift).

CEOs and development officers need to ensure that the money is available for stewardship. In organizations with low budgets, the engagement of board members and other volunteers as partners in the process can keep the budget under control. Often, they will host the event that keeps the relationship strong, or they will buy the tickets for several people to attend a performance or lecture. However, until stewardship is properly budgeted, it will never be regarded as an integral part of the development process;

and until it is regarded as an integral part of the process, it will not be internalized or practiced consistently.

GETTING PROGRAM STAFF TO UNDERSTAND THE VALUE OF STEWARDSHIP

As stated in Chapter 10, the involvement of program staff in donor and volunteer interaction is critical. It is equally important in the stewardship program. Program connection is key to engagement, and engagement is the pivot point in gaining and maintaining transformational givers. Burdening program staff with additional assignments is difficult; as with external marketing, the benefits of their involvement need to be conveyed.

Internal marketing of the development function is connected to stewardship. To gain the appropriate involvement of program staff, they must understand why it is important for them and for the organization to connect with donors. In some organizations this is not an issue; in others, it prevents the development of a healthy stewardship program. Here are some ideas for getting busy program staff involved:

1. Educate them about how *development*—the process of uncovering shared values—works (Grace, 1997). Link it to *fund-raising,* the process of providing opportunities for people to act on their values. Separate the functions and let them know that they would be effective participants in the development process merely by letting people see what they do in their work and that staff and volunteer leadership will take care of the fund-raising. Let them know that *stewardship*—the art and science of keeping people involved after they make a gift—is the best part of the development process. The commitment has been made; their job is to keep the commitment alive, which they do best by doing what they do and sharing the process or results with the investors.
2. Don't overburden them. A wise man once remarked, "I was my father's favorite son, so he made me do all the work." We do the same with our staff and our volunteers. Spread the opportunity throughout the organization. Don't waste staff people's time. The donor has already selected your organization as the best place to make a transforming gift. You just want to make sure that the donor can receive the kind of informed stewardship that builds confidence in his investment. If there are staff people who become cranky or uncooperative when asked to do this kind of outreach, don't involve them. Shift your strategy. Try to find other program

staff who can speak to the larger issues. Resistant staff people can quell donor enthusiasm and make them take their funding elsewhere.

3. Train them about interacting with donors. Don't assume that staff people are knowledgeable or comfortable with wealthy people. Many of them are not, and can be either shy around them or cynical about them. Fortunately, the widespread media attention to philanthropy has conveyed a much more human face to transformational donors. This is helping people who are inexperienced at working with wealthy people. They can see that these people care about the things they care about, and that the program person who works with developmentally delayed children and the person who invests in programs to help those children are in fact pursuing the same vision. This provides a stronger platform for building relationships.

4. Fit donor visits into regular programming schedules to prevent increasing the work burden for staff. If someone is coming from out of town, that may change the way in which the visit is handled. For the most part, however, try to fit the donor's visit into the program schedule.

5. Help program staff understand that these investors are not trying to control the programming through their gifts, but that they want to make an investment that will change the circumstances and outcomes of the issues they care about. Explain their partnership role, with the nonprofit and the community, in seeing to it that programs are delivered and effective. Concerns about "buying a seat on the board" or other ways that large investors may appear to exercise control must be viewed in the larger context of transformational giving: A major donor-investor in a nonprofit is going to want to have information about how their investment is performing and some involvement in its impact. This is one of the realities of transformational giving.

GAUGING THE EFFECTIVENESS OF YOUR STEWARDSHIP PROGRAM

The best gauge of the effectiveness of your stewardship program is the continued engagement of transformational and other key donors with your organization. Be sure you are tracking overall donor retention, as well as keeping up with the way your key investors are reacting and responding to your organization. Building institutional loyalty is best done in the context of how you are addressing the issues that really matter to your investors.

Detailed principles for creating, as well as steps for implementing, a full stewardship program can be found in *Beyond Fund-Raising* (Grace, 1997). There is a comprehensive chapter devoted to stewardship that can be a guide for those organizations new to this critical development practice.

Frame all of your stewardship, as you do all of your outreach, in the marketing principles described in the previous chapter.

New Strategies

Evaluating the Impact

of Philanthropy

In *High Impact Philanthropy*, evaluation is implicit. For nonprofits, donor-investors, and communities who partner for high impact philanthropy, accountability, evaluation, feedback, and visible results are essential.

Evaluation is a notoriously neglected but extremely important aspect of all development practices, particularly for transformational giving. To sustain the community/donor-investor/nonprofit organization partnership that will strengthen communities, you must find new ways to measure the impact of philanthropy.

Program evaluation, which varies from organization to organization depending on the type of service delivery, is the core of feedback to donors. Donor-investors want results, and evaluation allows nonprofits to quantify those results.

Internally, evaluation is a tool for program revision and modification; externally, evaluation is the way the nonprofit lets its investors know it is meeting the community needs expressed in its mission. Nonprofits want to convey their impact in the community, and the ways in which gifts to their organization made that impact possible. *Quantitative measures* (how many served, changes in clients or the community as a result of those services) stimulate continued donor involvement and support. *Qualitative measures* (stories and anecdotes) give life to the statistics, and offer the donor a way to tell others about the organization's impact. Program measurement is a special field, and not the subject of this book, except to the extent that it is required for effective donor-investor feedback. A commitment to accurate and timely evaluation is essential to good investor relations. One project in

Kenya, Africa, that is teaching and implementing appropriate technologies to encourage entrepreneurship, has an *impact monitor* for its projects. More nonprofits should think of such a position.

The focus for this chapter is the measurement of philanthropic impact. Although program evaluation is imbedded in all philanthropic evaluation, particular attention will be given to three key issues:

- Evaluating the philanthropic environment for the formation of important partnerships among nonprofit organizations, donor-investors, and communities
- Evaluating the philanthropic environment within the organization as a stimulus for transformational giving
- Evaluating the measurable impact of transformational giving in a geographic or issue-defined community and/or organization

VEHICLES FOR CONVEYING EVALUATION RESULTS: PROGRAMMATIC AND PHILANTHROPIC MEASURES

Programmatic and philanthropic evaluation have traditionally intersected in the reporting required by foundation and government funders. Program-directed grants require an accounting of the money spent and of the impact of the grant. Formal reports vary from a few pages for a local foundation to reams of forms required by some federal and state government programs. In these reports, attempts are made to convey the impact of the grant while complying with the fiduciary reporting requirements. In some cases, the evaluations provide an opportunity for organizations to do a survey of program delivery that can be used for other outreach purposes; other reports are limited in usefulness to the specific purpose for which they are written.

Nonprofit organizations that have vigorous and successful direct mail programs often use community-wide letters as a vehicle for reporting on their impact. The positive trend away from talking about organizational needs and focusing instead on community needs has brought a refreshing change of tone to these letters. Still largely unread and with poor response rates (0.8% from a "cold" list), these letters nonetheless offer an exercise in self-evaluation for nonprofits, requiring them to summarize their accomplishments and to position themselves as good investments.

Other opportunities for summary evaluations of accomplishments specifically related to particular grants or gifts arise constantly in organizations and can be used effectively for marketing or positioning the nonprofit while giving the donor needed feedback. These include

- Program brochures
- Donor recognition events
- Volunteer recognition events
- Newsletters
- Web sites
- Program proposals for new funding based on the successful investment of previous funding
- Board-meeting presentations by program staff who have benefited from the funding

In addition to providing valuable feedback to donors, these kinds of summary evaluations provide inspiration and information for volunteers in their informal (advocate) and formal (asker-advocate) roles. These summary evaluations—effective combinations of statistics and stories—are valuable marketing tools as well as effective reporting vehicles.

THE SPREAD OF PHILANTHROPY AND THE TRENDS IN INVESTMENT: THE BACKGROUND FOR EVALUATING COMMUNITY IMPACT

Noted by Alexis de Tocqueville (*Democracy in America*, 1831) as a unique aspect of American society from its very beginnings, the act of organizing in communities to help others has grown beyond America's borders. Private investors with a sense of global responsibility are beginning to strengthen a wide variety of geographic and issues-based communities around the world. Some of these are new, some are struggling but sturdy, others are vigorous and successful, and still others are seen as needed risk investments if change is going to occur. Although most investors prefer to invest in something that is already (or is sure to become) a success, the shift to an issues focus in philanthropy has led to venturesome long-term funding of organizations that have identified and are working to solve critical human, social, and educational problems. Particular among these is the investment in education.

Across America, and in countries like Nepal, China, and Mexico, there is a growing awareness of the need for greater investment in education.

In the past decade in America, the newest trend has been private investment in public education. Public school districts first began attracting private investment through the creation in California, Hawaii, Arizona, and elsewhere of independent foundations that raised private money for public education from their communities. Now, increasingly, the investment in K–12 education is direct, going right into the school, district, or classroom without benefit of the foundation. In some areas of America, for-profit corporations have taken over the business of educating children. This is outside the system of philanthropy, and is a serious indictment of the failure of communities to forge partnerships that effectively strengthen critical institutions. The swirl of activity in public primary and secondary education is matched by the degree of interest in higher education.

The investment in higher education in America and elsewhere in the late twentieth and early twenty-first centuries is monumental. Eight- and nine-figure gifts have transformed American public and private institutions. In the United Kingdom, major campaigns for Oxford and Cambridge universities set the pace decades ago; and CASE (the Council for Advancement and Support of Education) holds an ever-growing annual conference for schools and universities in the United Kingdom at which issues of philanthropy and investment are discussed by outside presenters and development teams. Education is the area to which much of the funding from new philanthropists has been given. It is seen as the means by which the greatest number of people can benefit from an investment: students, faculty, researchers, and, in the long term, the ideas and communities that will be affected by the work and involvement.

Investment in cultural institutions has flourished in museums for modern and contemporary art in San Francisco, London, and Prague; in massive renovations of natural history museums in New York and San Francisco; in private investment in the foundation to support the Guimet Museum of Asian art in Paris; and in Mexico, where noted artists Francisco Toledo and Rodolfo Morales have quietly reinvested the money they have made from their art into the conservation of historic buildings that promote the arts and arts education in the area surrounding Oaxaca and in other arts-related programs. In East Berlin, Germany, partitioned from the world and with a crumbling infrastructure until the wall came down in 1988, an architectural, cultural, and economic renaissance is taking place—and private investment in many of its institutions is growing.

In all kinds of institutions, all around the world, the need for private investment has soared. Global health needs have captured the Bill and

Melinda Gates Foundation's and other funders' passions even while the philanthropic funding of America's hospitals has been challenged by the changes in healthcare and in hospital ownership. Grass-roots organizations, previously unaware of their potential for transformational investment, are benefiting from multiple-year venture funding from concerned community leaders with a strong issues focus. Interest in educational and social issues in South and Southeast Asia command the time and attention of people from around the world. The recovery of Cambodia's cultural heritage at Angkor Wat has been strengthened by the partnership of the Cambodian government, the World Monuments Fund, and private investors. A donor wall stands near a new temple in Thailand, mirroring American recognition practices. The International Fund Raising Workshop, held annually in The Netherlands, has an ever-increasing enrollment from Europe, the United States, Asia, and other regions, and conducts intensive master classes on philanthropic issues that bind people from many cultures into a common view and practice of philanthropy.

EVALUATING THE IMPACT OF PHILANTHROPY

Individual projects are relatively easy to evaluate, but the long-term impact of the kind of philanthropic investment we've described here is only just beginning to be felt. In this new era of philanthropy, nonprofit organizations need to evaluate wide issues of philanthropic impact as the larger context for assessing specific programs and the grants and investments that have funded them. This is a critical role they play in the transformational partnership among communities, nonprofits, and donor-investors.

Nonprofits are uniquely positioned to assess the issues that inspire philanthropic participation. Through networking, a unique attribute of their role in community-building, they keep in touch with broader issues in the sector that can provide benchmarks by which to measure their own effectiveness. As experts in philanthropy, nonprofits need to provide communities and donor-investors with information that will lead to better analysis of community needs and more investment participation. This evaluation should have the *issue* at the core—homelessness, family planning, public education, elder abuse—not only the institution's progress in addressing that issue. The nonprofit sector, through its organizations, has a tremendous responsibility in the community-strengthening partnership with donor-investors and communities to evaluate, reassess, redesign, reinvent, and renew philanthropic endeavors.

PHILANTHROPY FOR THE TWENTY-FIRST CENTURY: STANDARDS FOR EVALUATING ITS IMPACT

We have been launched by the strength of philanthropic investment on a global initiative to strengthen communities through an effective partnership among nonprofit organizations, communities, and donor-investors. The key to the high impact of this philanthropy will be transformational giving, but it is the practice of philanthropy that needs to evaluate itself continually. A healthy philanthropic environment has a strong influence on transformational giving. When coupled with a robust economy and access to issues through institutions, it is the formula for investor, nonprofit, and community satisfaction.

Three sets of evaluation criteria follow. The first two provide guidelines for evaluating aspects of the philanthropic environment; the third provides specific measures for evaluating the impact of transformational gifts.

Evaluating the Philanthropic Environment for the Formation of Important Partnerships among Nonprofit Organizations, Donor-Investors, and Communities

Here are the key ingredients of a philanthropic environment that encourages and nurtures community partnerships (see Chapters 1 and 6):

1. An active, issues-focused network of nonprofits and umbrella agencies committed to exploring ways in which they can work together to identify and address issues and evaluate their progress
2. A commitment, by local and regional governmental agencies and nonprofits to assess and update information about community issues and needs on a continual basis and to publicize that information widely to the community, including potential and practicing donor-investors, professionals, and clients
3. A community that is informed about the philanthropic sector and the way in which it operates to strengthen communities

4. Consistent marketing of the impact of nonprofit activities on issues and ideas of significance in the community
5. Potential and practiced donor-investors who self-identify around specific issues—including overall community development—and are willing to become involved with others who share their values and concerns
6. A community—geographic or issues-based—that is capable of articulating its vision and enrolling others in it
7. A community in which the diversity of investors is honored and recognized, and the role that each plays in philanthropic achievement is viewed as important
8. People who are willing to give both time and money for philanthropic projects

Evaluating the Philanthropic Environment within the Organization as a Stimulus for Transformational Giving

Donor-investors look at these criteria when considering a transformational investment in an organization:

1. How closely the donor's and the organization's values match
2. The strength and quality of staff and board leadership, and the donor's confidence in them
3. How predominantly the organization has marketed itself as a key player in solving issues important to the donor-investor
4. How successful the organization has been or will be, or how urgent the issue is and what factors exist that justify a multiple-year risk investment
5. How informed staff and board are about the larger issues that provide context and meaning for the organization's activities
6. Who the key leaders are, and how they evidence their integrity and reputation
7. What the long-term benefits to the community will be
8. How well the investment will be managed
9. Future role(s) for the investor
10. What voice the investor will have in decision making about fund management or other aspects of the gift
11. How willing the organization is to conduct and report evaluations
12. How the donor will be treated relative to stewardship—whether he or she needs to be involved, be recognized, or be left alone.

To create an environment for transformational giving, these 12 criteria can serve as guide points for organizational evaluation.

Evaluating the Measurable Impact of Transformational Giving in a Geographic or Issue-Specific Community and/or Organization

Implicit in the word *transformational* is the idea that the gift will transform. As we have developed throughout this book, the transformation occurs at many levels: program, institution, donor, and community. The complexity of the concept of transformational giving should not detract from the fundamental simplicity of measuring its effectiveness from the standpoint of the gift itself.

Seven Evaluation Questions for Measuring the Impact of Transformational Gifts

1. Did it transform?
   a. At what levels?
   b. How has it transformed our organization?
   c. Has it transformed our community, and in what ways?
   d. How has it transformed the donor?
   e. Did it transform our community's ability to address the issue that was at the heart of the donor's gift?
   f. Has it transformed the community's perception of our organization?
   g. What impact has it had on the issue?
2. Can we keep this going?
   a. Do we want to keep this going, or was it a one-time effort?
   b. What resources would we need to keep it going?
   c. Is there another donor who will join the effort now that progress has been made?
3. Should we keep this going?
   a. Does it fit with our long-range plan and our mission?
   b. Is it still a priority?
   c. Did we solve the problem sufficiently so that we don't need such resources again?
   d. Does addressing the issue require continued investment?
4. Were costs well estimated, and did we manage them well?

a. If it was a capital project, did we manage the budget and keep the costs of the project and of fund-raising at an acceptable level?
b. Did we make appropriate adjustments during the course of the project and inform the investor about these adjustments to the project or the budget?
c. If we had to go back to the donor for additional funds, did we make our case well and provide the needed documentation?
d. If the transformational gift was for endowment, have we managed it well? If from a living donor, have we kept the donor informed? If from an estate, have we informed the family or provided appropriate recognition?

5. Did we involve the donor appropriately?
   a. If the donor wanted to be on the board, to be on a committee or a task force, or just to give advice and counsel in an ad hoc capacity, did we accept that request graciously?
   b. If the donor wanted to be left alone except for specific communications, did we honor that request?
   c. Was the recognition we provided what the donor wanted? Could we have done it better?
   d. Did we make an effort to accommodate reasonable requests from the donor for time or feedback, even if the requests were not always well-timed from our standpoint?

6. Will this gift be leverage for other gifts?
   a. How have we used this gift to inspire others?
   b. Has the donor been willing to make calls with us? Have we asked the donor to become an asker-advocate, or have we assumed that would not be a welcome task?
   c. How has our marketing around the impact of the gift been positioned so others see us as a strong investment?
   d. Have we marketed the impact of this gift in such a way that people see its broader impact on the community and understand the important partnership among our organization, the donor-investor, and the community?

7. Was/is our stewardship effective?
   a. Is the donor happy that he or she made the investment?
   b. Have we shown respect for the source and impact of the gift?
   c. Are we, as an organization, philosophically committed to stewardship of all donors, not just transformational donors?
   d. Has our stewardship of this donor included regular information about the impact of this gift not only on the organization, but on the community as well?

CONCLUSION

At every level, evaluation is a principal factor in community-building philanthropy and transformational giving. This broad view of the growth of philanthropy, together with the specific evaluation issues organizations and communities must ask themselves, provide valuable information for donor-investors who want to be involved.

Donor-investors have the responsibility to look for and help establish the environment for healthy philanthropy by having appropriate expectations for the performance and responsibility of nonprofits. Communities contribute to this environment by being effective partners that provide important information, assessment, and resources.

Evaluation is the center of the transformational giving loop. It is to be honored and implemented.

High Impact Philanthropy Timetable (HIPT)

A Quarterly Schedule Of Tasks To Achieve High Impact Philanthropy And Transformational Giving

The High Impact Philanthropy Timetable (HIPT) is the task manager for achieving the results we discuss in this book. Lay leaders and volunteers who give freely of their time to nonprofit organizations do not want to sit and talk, they want to act. A timetable gives all concerned a plan of action to achieve the goals we have set out for high impact philanthropy.

Quarterly	TO DO THIS QUARTER	RESPONSIBLE PERSON	✓
First	a. Governing board of nonprofit establishes High Impact Philanthropy Committee (HIPC)		
	b. HIPC sets goals: Both monetary and number of transformational givers to recruit		
	c. HIPC makes list of possible prospects		
	d. HIPC, nonprofit board of directors, and advisory committee establish link between their members and prospects		
	e. HIPC and professional staff set up research criteria and computer database		
	f. HIPC and staff begin research on each prospect		
	g. Based on linkage in item (d), assignments are made with lay leadership and prospects		
	h. High impact philanthropy case statement is written (see chapter 4)		
Second	a. Make initial appointments with prospects		
	b. Decide which staff person should accompany lay leader on appointments		
	c. Set up pre-appointment training session for each team		
	d. HIPC committee must have a list of all agency programmatic events		
	e. At initial meeting invite prospect to an appropriate agency programmatic event		
Third	a. Complete database program		
	b. Sort database for donors who have given a minimum gift during past three years, in an amount that would indicate a potential major donor-investor		
	c. If the breadth of donor research information is limited, consider purchasing private data from a commercial financial firm		
	d. Write a grant for possible funding of private research data		
Fourth	a. Ask each prospect for a gift		
	b. Interview prospects who have dropped out of stewardship process; committee needs to know why they are no longer interested		
	c. Evaluate stewardship program (see chapter 12)		

Special Resources

The resources listed in this section will assist your agency and help it produce the transformational gifts that will help your organization realize its goals. This appendix will cover two areas:

- Organizations to contact for information about fund-raising and non-profit management
- A bibliography of texts that the authors consider to be the most helpful to an agency in developing their fund-raising plans.

PROFESSIONAL ORGANIZATIONS FOR NONPROFIT AGENCIES

American Association of Fund-Raising Counsel (AAFRC)
25 West 43rd Street, Suite 820
New York, NY 10036
Telephone (212) 354-5799
AAFRC publishes the annual report, "Giving USA," that measures the state of American Philanthropy.

Association for Healthcare Philanthropy (AHP)
313 Park Avenue, Suite 400
Falls Church, VA 22046
Telephone (703) 532-6243
Website: www.go-ahp.org

Independent Sector
1828 I Street, N.W.
Washington, DC 20036
Telephone (202) 223-8100
Web site: www.indepsec.org

Association of Fund Raising Professionals (formally National Society of Fund-Raising Executives [NSFRE])
1101 King Street, Suite 700
Alexandria, VA 22314-2967
Telephone (703) 684-0410
Web site: www.nsfre.org
NSFRE advances philanthropy through education, training, and advocacy; certifies professional fund raisers (CFREs); and is the largest professional fund-raising association in the United States. Check the web site for the location of your local chapter.

National Center for Nonprofit Boards
2000 'L' Street, Suite 510
Washington, DC 20036-4907
Web site: www.ncnb.org
NCNB is the site to visit if your organization wants to stay up to date on nonprofit board developments.

The Foundation Center
79 Fifth Avenue
New York, NY 10003-3076
Web site: www.fdncenter.org
Telephone 1-800-424-9836
The Foundation Center is a national service organization that provides a source of information on foundations and corporate giving. The Center maintains libraries around the country. Call their 800 number for the collection nearest your community.

NONPROFIT NEWSPAPERS

The Chronicle of Philanthropy
Web site: www.philanthropy.com

NonProfit Times
Web site: www.nptimes.com

Contributions
Web site: www.contributionsmagazine.com

BIBLIOGRAPHY AND RECOMMENDED READING

Downs, Alan. 2000. *The Fearless Executive*. Saranac Lakes, NY: AMACOM.

Friedman, Thomas L. 1999. *The Lexus and the Olive Tree: Understanding Globalization*. New York: Farrar, Straus and Giroux.

Grace, Kay Sprinkel. 1997. *Beyond Fund-Raising—New Strategies for Nonprofit Innovation and Investment*. New York: John Wiley & Sons, Inc.

Harris, Thomas. 1999. *International Fund-Raising for Not-for-Profits: A Country-by-Country Profile*. New York: John Wiley & Sons, Inc.

Johnston, Michael. 1999. *The Fund Raiser's Guide to the Internet*. New York: John Wiley & Sons, Inc.

Levy, Barbara R., et al. (eds.). 1996. *The NSFRE Fund-Raising Dictionary*. New York: John Wiley & Sons, Inc.

Putnam, Robert D. 2000. *Bowling Alone: The Collapse and Revival of an American Community*. New York: Simon & Schuster.

Rosenberg Jr., Claude. 1994. *Wealthy and Wise: How You and America Can Get the Most Out of Your Giving*. New York: Little, Brown & Company, 1994.

Wendroff, Alan L. 1999. *Special Events: Proven Strategies for Nonprofit Fund-Raising*. New York: John Wiley & Sons, Inc.

Index

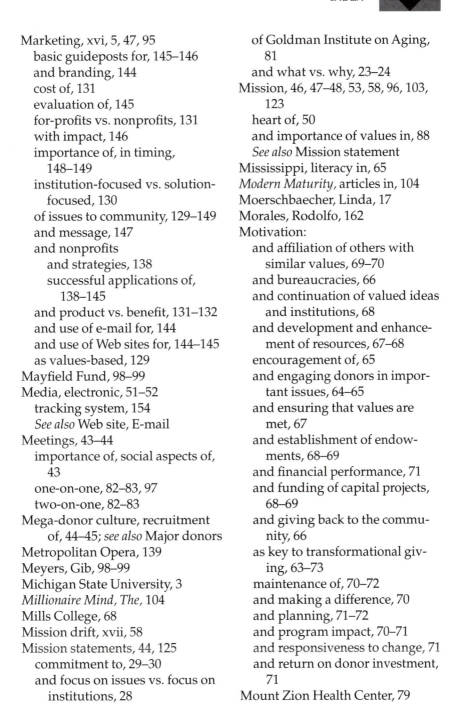